A RAMBLER'S ROAD TO THE LAW

By

Rebecca A. Taylor

Contents

Acknowledgments

Thank you to everyone I have ever learned from in my legal career who taught me to become a better legal professional, whether those lessons were good or bad.

Thank you to Brion Blackwelder, Richard Grosso, and Joel Mintz; through your dedication to environmental law you showed me some of the best of what lawyering can be.

Love and thanks to Mom, Chuck, my husband Jim and son Carl; I am a lucky and blessed lady, daughter and mom to have you all as my family.

I praise God for giving me the calling, passion, wherewithal and knowledge to write.

People will tell you where they've gone

They'll tell you where to go

But till you get there yourself you never really know

↺ Joni Mitchell, "Amelia"

Introduction

••••••••••••••••••••••

Long before the unemployment and economy crisis began, I never saw job security as a sure thing. Maybe that's because I began my legal career as a temp. I grew accustomed to floating around, constantly experiencing different personalities and environments. I somehow never entered a job envisioning it as my home for the next twenty or thirty years. As a result of my rather nomadic career-style, I have had the benefit of learning from many different people.

My working life began when I was about eleven. I would mow our huge lawn and my dad would then give me $30.00 for an hour of riding lessons. I also worked down at the local food Co-op to earn "work credit" to earn discounts off grocery purchases, as any customer could do. The work credit could then be sold to others and this proved to be another source of riding lesson cash flow for me.

Through my combined experience in manual labor, food service, military and the law, I have experienced many different personalities, ways of thinking and doing things. I believe these adventures eventually gave me a greater understanding of my legal responsibilities and overcoming the hurdles one must navigate on the way to becoming a lawyer.

Today of course, we have reached an economic climate which may cause job seekers to experience nomadic careers for a time, perhaps not by choice as I have. I thought I was too good for certain jobs until a very wise friend of mine told me to get off my high horse. I have always treasured his advice - though, as a result of his words I entered unfamiliar and scary worlds, I was also set free in many ways.

In writing this book, I hope to pass on some encouragement and lessons from my road to others seeking a legal career, whether that is as an attorney, paralegal, secretary, or file clerk. In some positions, even attorneys may find that their responsibilities overlap with some of these legal staff. You may start out as a support staff member, then move into another position, perhaps become an attorney. Many of the concepts and experiences I share here relate to those of someone new to the legal industry or those of a young, inexperienced lawyer; however, there are techniques and nuggets which any legal professional or aspirant can take and integrate into their work, however it may suit them. I share facts and hard-learned knowledge I wish I had known before embarking on my own voyage.

I also take into account the different circumstances law career seekers must face today, as opposed to what I experienced when I took my first paralegal job. I recognize the harsh realities of the economy today and how it also impacts students' ability to obtain educational loans. Yet

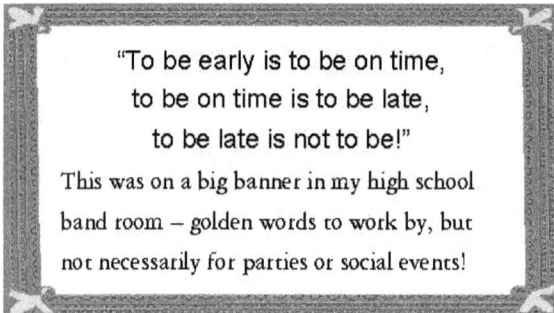

> "To be early is to be on time,
> to be on time is to be late,
> to be late is not to be!"
> This was on a big banner in my high school band room – golden words to work by, but not necessarily for parties or social events!

there are still many of us who experience that burning conviction that a legal career is our destiny. Where there's a will, there's a way. You may just need more patience. Of course most of us like instant gratification. But you are not likely to find that kind of success in law school. For anyone looking to become a lawyer these days, an extreme amount of due diligence is needed. A prospective law student should ask herself questions such as these: What kind of legal career do I want? Do I want to make it into a top law firm and if so, am I willing to do what it takes to make top grades and obtain entrance to Law Review and Moot Court? Is the big law firm life-style what I really want? What can I do to start building my résumé before and while I'm in law school? Do I want to have my own business and if so, what resources do I have to launch a business? If I don't have any resources now, what can I do to get them? Do I understand just how much law school will cost? How will I pay for it and how will that affect my life after I've finished school?

Ask yourself these questions, and more - all the questions you can think of about how to reach your goal in law. And do it! Also, life and career goals can often be moving targets, so what your goal is today may not be the case in five years, a year, or even less. Much depends on whether you take the employee or business owner route. Our school system doesn't always tell you this - but this is a very important issue for you to consider. To do so, you must educate yourself until all of your questions are answered.

Chapter 1:   Is a Lawyer Born or Made?

How does one know if he will make a good lawyer?   This can be hard to determine.   There are attorneys who may be considered very talented but have some tragic flaw which deteriorates their level of service or even leads to their undoing. There are other lawyers who may not be considered especially smart or popular amongst their peers but have the determination and ethics which will give them staying power and success in the long run.

Before Depositions, Draft a Script of As Many Questions as Possible That You Want Answered

Some people have predetermined conceptions of who should become a lawyer, such as those who are loud, gregarious, opinionated, smart, or like to argue. However someone who is shy and withdrawn but is hard-working, conscientious and willing to learn could very well outshine a slick type-A personality.   A shy person could shudder at the thought of getting up and arguing before a judge or entire court, but it is simply a skill which can be learned and improved upon with practice and experience, which is not necessarily the same skill as being a great public speaker or orator.

At the end of the day, it doesn't really matter whether you are naturally shy or outgoing because arguing in front of people in court, meeting with and advising clients, and public speaking at seminars are all skills that can be learned with practice. What really matters is your determination to learn and your integrity. Know where you stand on things. Are you willing to sacrifice your family life for work, and to what extent? Will you do something unethical if everyone else is doing it, or perhaps if you are given an ultimatum to follow shady orders or pack your bags? Are you just in the legal profession for the money - if so, no matter how much money you make, it may never be enough. All of these questions raise issues that can wear away at you in a career which is filled with potential landmines.

A law professor once said to my class that "You are never going to be any smarter than you are now -

you can learn new skills and gain experience but your intelligence level pretty much stays the same." I don't agree with this. First of all, your experiences and skills help define and complement your intelligence level. For example, you could be faced with a decision on whether to file a motion for default against your opposing party. Without the benefit of experience, I once decided to proceed with such a motion but in hindsight it was not the smartest decision I ever made. Some attorneys would probably have called it flat out dumb, not just a rookie mistake. I had scheduled my motion for default for hearing, just so eager to end the case in our favor, and opposing counsel didn't show. Finally he called the judge's chambers asking for me, begging me to cancel the hearing. My desperation to just get this monkey of a case off my back was greater than my willingness to work with opposing counsel and show him a professional courtesy that years later, I would have granted without question, however begrudgingly. I shouldn't just have considered the law on default judgments and how easily they can be overturned because courts prefer to decide disputes on their merits. I should have considered the consequences of my actions on my relations with opposing counsel, which were already extremely antagonistic. Many attorneys, particularly young ones, think that if they play hardball on every issue, regardless of the propriety of their actions, they will gain respect and not just be seen as a "freshout." You can learn the hard way that doing so will just turn your colleagues against you when you could be building your database of professional contacts. However you could have the foresight and wisdom to realize this before learning from the school of hard knocks, which I then lacked.

What is intelligence anyway? To me, it's a combination of wisdom, knowledge, experience and common sense. Because of this, someone who gets straight-As in school but is only book smart does not necessarily make a great lawyer. The practice of law largely depends on common sense, or street smarts as well. It takes common sense to know the practical consequences of your actions, or to avoid wasting valuable time on trivial activities, such as arguing with opposing counsel. Being a good lawyer also means having empathy for and being able to relate to your clients, and being a good listener.

True legal intelligence usually cannot be learned in college or law school. Institutions of higher learning usually do not employ enough practical applications of information for that. If education was delivered properly, most of us would not so quickly forget virtually everything we learned in law school. To illustrate, I was in the Army for little over a year, but I was constantly engaged in training and education of a different kind. It was not necessarily academic or intellectual training, but often just as important, complex or crucial, as quite often your life might depend on it. I remember much more about my education in the Army than I do from all of law school. From the three brutal weeks under an August sun in Fort Benning, Georgia, I learned how to properly pack my parachute, how to do a roll/drop landing, how to hold my arm along the static line as I waited for a jump, how to pull the emergency rip-cord in the event the chute did not open on its own, and a Jody call about the black hat/old lady/airborne instructor to which we would often run in cadence. Why do I still remember so much about a three-week training over ten years later? It was a school of doing, of full engagement, where you paid attention and learned or you could die.

It's not that I think your life depends on paying attention in school or that it even should, but if there was a great deal more of practical application of cases and exercises we as attorneys might remember more of that education which often costs us 100K or more. I am not an educator and do not profess to offer the best concepts as to practically convey the messages of legal opinions. One idea, however, might be to make a game out of it. Have some students act out the events of the case in a skit. Have some students act as judges and others role play the attorneys in the case, reconstruct the arguments, improvise upon them and see whether, after each side has made its presentation, whether the class still agrees with the original verdict or thinks a different result should have been obtained.

One of my former bosses once said to me, quite seriously, that I should demand my money back from my law school because it had not adequately prepared me for the real world of law practice. Ironically, he was an alum of my same school, having graduated over a generation prior. But many lawyers I have known have echoed these sentiments, that law school does not offer enough practical law practice skills and instead focuses on abstract concepts of law, such as class discussions of cases which occurred hundreds of years ago in England, instead of focusing more on real-life applications of legal problems in the world around us, and hands-on approaches on how to solve them.

Chapter 2: Cost of Higher Education

My main attraction to a legal career was the prospect of good, solid income. The student loans I would have to incur were an afterthought, taken for granted as part of the means to the end. For most students today, college and graduate school are still not possible without loans. However, the availability of loans and jobs by which graduates may repay these loans has been decimated by the recent economic crises. It is anyone's guess as to how long the current economic and job market will last. Thus, the analysis one might consider in deciding to become an attorney today may differ from such a consideration in years past.

Many people seek the legal profession expecting to attain a high salary. Most law graduates will eventually find jobs as attorneys, but many attorney salaries today still start between $40,000 or lower to the mid-$60Ks annually. While these may seem like respectable salaries, often they do not go far after the attorney has finished paying her student loans for the month, many of which carry exorbitant interest rates.

In the end, most attorneys I have known end up just like most other employees, living paycheck to paycheck. Their debt too, like other employees, seems to rise commensurate with their salary.

When I made plans for college, I did not give much thought to student loans; to me, they were simply a given in pursuing a higher education. Back then, there was no issue in my mind as to credit concerns or whether I would be granted an educational loan or not. Obviously, I had to pay for my education somehow and it just seemed like something everyone had to do (short of the independently wealthy). Thus, I did not give any thought to factors such as interest rates, term of the loan, choice of lenders, etc. I regretted this decision years later as my monthly student loan payments of over $500.00 were covering little more than interest. It is a horrible thing to fear never being debt-free and being an indentured servant to lenders for most of, if not all of your life.

Of course, the prospect of being saddled by a debt tantamount to a mortgage without the benefit of owning tangible real property can serve as an impetus for a law student to do whatever it takes to qualify for jobs at the top firms, often carrying the highest salaries. The idea then would be to have more money with which to pay the student loans off faster. However, by the time someone is done with law school they could very well owe $100,000.00 for their J.D. degree alone, not even counting costs for undergraduate school, housing, books, living expenses, etc. For example, at my alma mater Nova Southeastern University Shepard Broad Law Center, the annual tuition for full-time day students is currently $32,750.00.[1]   For a three year program, if such students pay for their education via loans, they will owe $98,250.00 at the conclusion of their studies, not even including interest. I was charged interest at the rate of twelve percent per annum by Sallie Mae. So if a student is charged twelve percent interest on a $98,250.00 loan amortized over thirty years, he will incur monthly payments of $1,010.61 and the total amount required to pay off the loan over thirty years will be $363,820.28, almost four times as much as the original amount borrowed.

---

[1] http://nsulaw.nova.edu/students/prospective/fees.cfm, as of June 22, 2011.

So, even if a law student is lucky enough to obtain a high-paying job following law school, she will still have a sizeable debt to pay every month for many years. To pay student loans off in full, as with any other sizeable debt, is best accomplished with consistent income. In this day and age, job security does not exist in the sense it perhaps did for our parents or the lucky few. My husband held down a job as a golf course maintenance worker for about thirty-two years before retiring to take care of our son so I could go back to my attorney job. We figured that his income would be little more than the cost of sending our son to daycare, so it seemed more efficient to have him be the one to stay home. Though my husband's only degree is from high school and he just completed a few college courses, he can boast a career record that many lawyers and other professionals can only dream about today – over three decades with the same company. If lawyers were assured this kind of job longevity, then the prospect of paying back over hundreds of thousands of dollars in loans would probably not seem so daunting.

A recent New York Times article asks the contemporaneously relevant question of "Is Law School a Losing Game?"[2] The central premise of this article is that the statistical data on how many law school graduates are employed within a given time after graduation and at what pay rate is misleading, and that law graduates' true financial circumstances today may leave them as indentured servants to their loans for the rest of their lives. A necessary tenet of this argument seems to be that law graduates aspire to become employees rather than business owners. This is not necessarily the case, but certainly the mindset that most students of American higher education are indoctrinated to have. Taking the article's assumption that most law students do seek jobs with blue chip law firms paying an annual starting salary of $160,000.00 or higher, it is certainly true that most such students may lose at this game, given that the qualifications for such positions require top grades from a prestigious school.

When You First Start Work On a Case, Make a Memo to File Summarizing All The Facts and Law You Know So Far

---

[2] David Segal, Is Law School a Losing Game?, NEW YORK TIMES, January 8, 2011.

In reality, the statistics consider a law graduate to be "employed" for the sake of the survey even if she is employed in a non-legal industry, such as waiting tables, cashiering or any other job. Many students were lured to law school by promises of a $160,000.00 median salary, believing that shouldering hundreds of thousands of dollars in debt was a prudent business risk in light of the employment prospects.

Not surprisingly, the data appears to not be so much for the benefit of aspiring lawyers, but for the law schools. As Mr. Segal notes, these institutions are "cash cows"; a lucrative hustle for the schools' owners, faculty and professors. The overhead costs for running a law school are miniscule compared with the revenue gained from the exorbitant student tuition. This article observes that twenty-five additional students might be added to an enormous lecture hall without the necessity of hiring another professor, while perhaps millions of dollars in additional tuition revenue goes straight to the law school's bottom line.

The financial investment for law school is often pitched as prudent and worthwhile to students, as they are led to believe an attorney job with the requisite recompense and longevity to conquer their debt will be a natural result of a law degree. Meanwhile, the only ones who invariably win are those whose incomes rise proportionately with the law school's profits.

I disagree with some of the aforementioned article's inherent assumptions, such as that most students seek to become employees of other lawyers or law firms. Another assumption is that attorneys who take jobs in the temporary legal business are unlikely to gain permanent law firm associate positions. The article claims that as you work as a legal temp and continue to age, by the time you seek candidacy as a permanent associate, you will be considered too old to assimilate into a "slave labor" culture.

Granted, the economy is starkly opposite now, but in the late '90s temporary legal work constituted the entirety of my relatively lucrative income, as discussed in Chapter 4. From what I have seen, experience is experience, no matter where it comes from, as long as it serves a potential employer's purposes. I believe that most prospective employers' main goal is to hire a competent producer who possesses the sufficient experience to hit the ground running and get results immediately with minimal hand-holding. You can get that experience just as well on temporary assignments as you can on "permanent" ones (and in this day and age, permanent rarely means that). It is not the duration of a position that really matters, but the substance, quality and depth of the work.

For example, while in the Army, which for many is a career endeavor, a soldier passes through numerous schools where specific skills are learned. I signed up for Airborne School, which lasted for three weeks in Fort Benning, Georgia. I learned to execute a life-threatening maneuver, static line parachute jumping, in three weeks. Yet this experience made me Airborne-qualified, earned me my wings and gained my entrance into the famed 82d Airborne Unit at Fort Bragg, North Carolina.

Take Copies of Documents To Hearings, Not Originals if Possible

Another example, in a legal context, is the pro-bono summer internship I performed at the Palm Beach Circuit Court for less than two months (discussed further in Chapter 9). Within a few weeks, I had seen almost every issue one could probably encounter in reviewing and responding to pro se criminal defendant post-conviction relief motions. I spent my days carefully reading these motions, researching the law cited therein, finding the law which would tell the whole story and what action should be taken next; i.e., whether to sustain the punishment imposed against the defendant or hold further proceedings in the matter. I was essentially in the temporary legal business with this internship, but this experience became an invaluable addition to my résumé, as my next employer knew some of the judges I had worked with and I received a glowing letter of recommendation from one of them.

Furthermore, I was eventually engaged for what was meant to be a temporary attorney assignment of about a week, but which eventually led to an offer of permanent employment, my associate position discussed further in Chapter 12. I started out with a very clerical task which involved going into the file room myself, with no secretary to assist me, and painstakingly going through each file myself to cull the necessary data to add to my report.

With every temporary assignment I have ever had, I have always taken the approach that in my every day work, I am being evaluated by management as to whether I would make a good permanent employee, and additional work is always a tremendous compliment. It is basically a buy signal; they are curious as to the extent of my skills, how much else I can help them with and how much burden I can take off their plate, which is a boon to any coworker.

When I completed the assignment within a week, my supervisor indicated that the next day would probably be my last, but she saw the look on my face and that I was serious about wanting more work. Sometimes it is not necessary to say too much to let your supervisor know you want to stay on; other times you should spell it out, but at all costs let them know you want to help as much as possible.

So, I disagree with the suggestion that law students or attorneys should not take temporary work for fear that it could disqualify them from permanent positions. This is not to say that some firms or employers might have a derisive view of such work – but then again no candidate is right for every job. But I have learned over my career that all relevant experience is good, regardless of the duration. You might have worked on a specific issue for only a few days or weeks, but you can discuss the extent of your knowledge and expertise regarding that issue in an interview, and show a prospective employer how exactly you can use these skills to hit the ground running.

While on one hand I take a devil's advocate approach to this article, I agree with many of its points. It serves no aspiring lawyer's purpose to naïvely ignore the high cost of a legal education and the frequent difficulty in finding income sufficient to pay down the attendant student loans. But legal jobs are out there; though you may not be able to work in your field of choice right away. My whole mission in going to law school at first was to practice environmental law, but I have not held one such position as a licensed attorney. I had to take work in general litigation, which I initially found unremarkable and insignificant, as this is what I thought most lawyers did; what difference did one more make? But the bills were waiting to be paid and the job market has always been portrayed to me as fierce, even in the now halcyon days of the late '90s New York City economy. I have always approached a serious job search as a game which I intended to play and win – sending out the right résumé, finessing the interview and approaching each interview with the intention of getting the job, whether or not I really wanted it. I was happy to start work as a practicing attorney, even if I was just part of the rat race and not serving my higher aspirations to protect the environment.

I also did not hesitate to take legal support staff positions when I deemed necessary. To put it bluntly, many attorneys need to get over themselves when it comes to clerical duties. Some attorneys will not so much as deign to retrieve a file, their mail, or even a cup of coffee themselves. Other attorneys may not have a secretary to wait on them hand and foot but will resist doing any task they feel is beneath them, such as answering phones, drafting their own letters, organizing their office, doing reasonable amounts of filing, scanning a document in, making a calendar entry, etc. Knowing how to do these tasks and actually doing them can only make you a better lawyer. It will teach you organizational skills, you will have better control over your calendar and to-do list, and you will have a better understanding of the entire legal process instead of just operating in a haughty bubble.

Taking support work at first will at least get your foot in the door, perhaps at the same law firm where you perform these clerical functions. Plenty of people in an industry have worked their way from the ground up and only prospered from it. You should not be concerned as to whether your colleagues will lose respect for you simply because you are in a support position. If you are good at what you do, you will make their jobs easier and your positive reputation will grow, potentially leading to an attorney position at the same firm, or at least a positive reference which will aid your career advancement.

Mr. Segal's article reiterates the need for aspiring lawyers to approach their education with eyes wide open to the financial reality of undertaking this pursuit, and to pursue all avenues to lessen the financial burden they will face upon graduation. If a student has the luxury of time, perhaps she can put savings aside for a number of years to assist with the cost. I once met one law student who was a real estate agent, made several lucrative commissions during the real estate boom and was able to pay for law school that way. We no longer have the luxury of that economy but there are still ways to make money in real estate, if approached the right way. I am not a financial advisor by any means but I have had the opportunity to meet a number of successful real estate investors. If done correctly, real estate can be one of the best hobbies for generating cash for all manner of pursuits.

For example, if an investor acquires a rehab property through a short sale, fixes it up a bit then resells it, she may be able to realize a profit if the numbers are right. This of course is harder to execute than it was in the housing boom, but feasible in the right circumstances. Other investors seek to purchase commercial property and obtain the constant flow of rental income. The more you can do yourself when it comes to certain steps, such as property repairs, management, accounting and marketing, the better off you are rather than having to pay someone to do these things for you and have these costs eat away at your return on investment (ROI).   Other professional services, such as legal, tax advice and title searches should not be performed by unqualified individuals; paying the professionals is often a necessary and prudent investment towards the success of your primary venture.

You should also leave no stone unturned in seeking scholarships and grants, monies given to you to spend on educational costs which you do not have to pay back. Many of these are based upon merit and/or need. If you are lucky enough to be wealthy but have still achieved excellent grades in school, then you may still receive merit-based aid. If you lack the money to pay for school yourself, you may qualify for need-based aid, and possibly merit awards as well if you also have the requisite grades.

Grant money may be classified under several categories: student-specific, subject-specific, degree level and minority.[3] Below are just a few examples of financial aid which students may pursue.

- ❖ **The Pell Grant**[4]
  - ➤ Designed to assist low-income students.
  - ➤ Students may apply for the Pell Grant by completing the Free Application for Federal Student Aid (FASFA).[5]
  - ➤ Award amounts are based on a student's Estimated Family Contribution (EFC), whether a student will be full or part-time, and how much time the student plans to participate in scholastic programs.
  - ➤ The maximum amount of Pell Grants in recent years has been about $4,000.00.
- ❖ **Federal Supplemental Educational Opportunity Grant (FSEOG)**[6]

---

[3] http://www.collegescholarships.org/grants/
[4] http://www.collegescholarships.org/grants/pell.htm
[5] http://www.fafsa.ed.gov/
[6] http://www2.ed.gov/programs/fseog/index.html

> Like the Pell Grant, FSEOG provides financial aid to low income students at approximately 4,000 participating postsecondary institutions.

> School administrators have substantial flexibility in determining the amount of FSEOG awards.

> FSEOG priority is given to those students with "exceptional need"; i.e., students who are already eligible for a Pell Grant and have the lowest EFCs.

> After completing the FASFA, students will be notified if they are eligible for FSEOG aid without the need for additional applications.[7]

❖ **The National Science & Mathematics Access to Retain Talent Grant (National SMART Grant)[8]**

> The National SMART Grant is available during the third and fourth years of undergraduate study (or fifth year of a five-year program) to at least half-time students who receive the Federal Pell Grant and who major in physical, life, or computer sciences, mathematics, technology,

---

[7] http://www.fseog.com/fseog-application.shtml

[8] http://studentaid.ed.gov/PORTALSWebApp/students/english/SmartGrants.jsp

engineering or a critical foreign language; or non-major single liberal arts programs.

➢ Students must hold and maintain at least a 3.0 GPA in their major.

➢ Students may receive up to $4,000.00 both their third and fourth years, or last year of a five-year program of study.

Chapter 3: College

When did I first think I wanted to become a lawyer? Probably not too long after I realized I wasn't going to be a detective like Nancy Drew. I was always thrilled by the late '80s series, kept on my toes for the next month's book, and would usually rip right through one in about two hours. Naturally I started questioning how one could become a detective and was eventually told that you had to become a police officer first. I was not inspired by this prospect and started considering other career options.

My dad, a professional bassoonist, persisted until I begrudgingly began to take up his instrument. The bassoon eventually grew on me and my proficiency grew. Before I knew it, I was offered a full scholarship to enter the University of Delaware's music program. I had been weighing my options between a career in music or law.

I had already made up my mind to pursue law, but music proved to be the vehicle to my school of choice. I was accepted to Rutgers' Mason Gross School of the Arts, though I had been rejected by Rutgers College. After one year as a music major and finishing with a 3.5 G.P.A., I was accepted as a transfer student by Rutgers College. Though Rutgers College had no specific pre-law program, it has always carried positive weight on my résumé.

It turned out my scheme had worked; using music and my proficiency therein as a vehicle to good grades, which were the tools I needed to enter my school of choice. I could not help but consider a permanent career in music while studying bassoon performance, as that was the plan under which my training operated. I had always loved music and performance of it; I had grown up around music and had enjoyed playing alone and in groups for years. However, I had many other interests too and I tended to be a "Jill of All Trades" – knowing a bit about everything but keeping everything fun, not taking anything too seriously to the point that I worked on something to the exclusion of all else. It did not take me too long to realize that if I wanted to become a professional musician, I would ultimately have to devote myself to music and make it the sole focus of my life. I was drawn to too much else, especially having arrived in a scene of endless possibilities, new friends and more freedom than I had ever experienced before.

Even before I was caught between these two career choices, I took my first employed position at the age of fourteen. My dad was constantly urging me to work, earn money so I could buy the things I wanted myself, and so he could keep me busy (thereby saving himself and my mom from my complaints of boredom around the house). Food and cooking were already hobbies and professional pursuits in my house. My mom had her own restaurant and did private catering. My brother would go to chef school and hold sous-chef positions at many fine restaurants. My sister would cultivate knowledge of wines and be a server at a number of high-end Manhattan eateries. Together with the wide availability of work in the fast-food industry and my family's predisposition toward food service, I became a University of Delaware dining hall worker in my high school freshman year. I continued working in the dining halls until the summer before leaving for

Rutgers, at which point I worked in the downtown Roy Rogers.

I did not get into my college of choice on my first try, so it is unclear what impact my employment history had on my college applications. For the most part, my grades and SAT score just weren't where they needed to be for Rutgers College's criteria as an incoming freshman. But many colleges look favorably upon working students, even if they hold jobs other than in their desired fields.[9] Admission staff look favorably upon students who do not just sit idle or party the summer away, develop their work ethic and reduce the cost of education burden which descends on these students and perhaps more so, their families. One director of admissions "provided the reassuring words that some of the best personal essays she'd read were the result of a summer working in fast food." And admissions faculty respect this work, some even to the point that they are perturbed by a candidate's essay efforts to explain away and justify having taken work in an allegedly inferior line of work.

---

[9] Lily Altavena, When A Part-Time Job Is Your Extracurricular Activity, NEW YORK TIMES, July 6, 2011.

Some colleges may offer a specific pre-law major or study program. This was not the case at Rutgers College; those interested in law were simply advised to choose a major which involved a good deal of reading and writing. In retrospect, I would have chosen my major on other factors based on what I know now. For example, I would have thought more about whether my ultimate goal was to become an employee or a business owner. I cannot remember either me or my class, as high school, college or law students, ever being asked whether we wanted to work for others or for ourselves; my entire education seemed designed to prepare me to become an employee. Now I know this is not the only option, but it was until over ten years after graduating from college that I received any training in business and sales.

Naturally, large corporations and other business owners need employees, cash rules, and big business has great influence over how students are educated in this country. After all, if we were all taught to believe we could become business owners, who would be left to work for us? The mandatory employee trainee program which seems to predominate in education fails to take into account that many people would rather be employees by choice. Fears that we would run out of employees seem misplaced. For example, I began working in the fast food service industry at the age of fourteen, but I knew my career would not ultimately lie in this field. How many people working as servers, waitresses and cooks plan to make a career out of it? Often, we use jobs as stepping stones. Some people do enjoy fulfilling careers in food service for many years, and no disrespect to the food service industry is meant, as I come from a family of chefs, catering and restaurant ownership. My point is that sometimes we begin in one place, and end somewhere completely different.

So, I might have considered business-oriented majors, as it was conceivable to me then that I might want to have my own law practice one day, though I had no idea how that might actually play out. I also might have thought more about what specific field of law I would want to practice. For example, I became interested in the environment and learning how to protect it at a young age. Perhaps if I had taken more courses in science, biology and geology, I would have acquired a more intimate knowledge and reverence for that which I sought to protect. As it stands today, in my multitudes of legal assignments and positions, I have never been employed in an environmental law capacity. Perhaps if I had studied different majors, I would have discovered more opportunities and made more connections in the environmental industry, leading to the sort of position in public interest advocacy I had envisioned.

For many students, practical knowledge and doing is a better way of learning than passively ingesting information from books and regurgitating it back in the professor's preferred form. I would have also begun to work on job skills lawyers use day to day, and perhaps joined the debate team or mock trial teams to that end. I also would have attended court hearings and proceedings occasionally so that I could see attorneys from all different professions in action.

A prospective law student should latch on to any opportunities to experience life as a lawyer does, including both the good and bad parts. If your college provides opportunities to hone necessary skills to lawyering, jump at those chances.   Southwestern

College has a Pre-Law Student Association which provides students with an "Attorney Alumni mentoring program, LSAT preparation, mock trial and debating activities and a curriculum that develops written, oral and analytical skills to insure success in law school and a career in law."[10] It is not enough to just research well, write good college papers and get good writing grades. A prelaw student should practice just like a lawyer (in the educational context only of course), which necessarily includes constant engagement in oral persuasiveness, presentations of argument, knowing what it is like to meet with a scared and frantic client, being overwhelmed with deadlines, and yes, even facing antagonistic opposing counsel and threats of sanctions.

Reading and Writing

 One necessary skill set to lawyering I was able to develop further in college was of course, reading and writing. I had already done this for years

---

[10] http://www.sckans.edu/undergraduate/political-science/pre-law/.

for fun. Writing had become a way for me to work things out; planning, understanding what I was feeling, a way to capture pieces of life as they flowed by, like driftwood in a river. Sometimes in college I just threw things together, writing papers in a crash overnight cram session, knowing I would probably just squeak by with a C and I was okay with that.

Other times, I threw my heart and soul into a project and I saw greatness in my own writing. For one American Studies class, my professor had us watch "Yellow Submarine" and analyze in a paper such questions as what the "Blue Meanies" symbolized. At times in college I felt like I was channeling the spirit and consciousness of people my age in the 1960s, and tried as hard as I could to picture myself at Woodstock – the sights, tastes, sounds, smells... It was from that place that I set down to work on the Yellow Submarine project. I no longer have that paper, but I remember writing about how the Blue Meanies represented the opposition to those in search of peace, an end to the wars, and unity through music, love, art and creativity. I wrote about the so-called flower children and how they seemed to be in the midst of a cultural, artistic and revolutionary renaissance. My teacher gave me an A+ on the paper. He left our papers outside his door for the students to collect at the conclusion of the class term, and he expressed profuse praise in his written comments on my paper, saying he could see jewels in my writing. This encouragement, together with my mom's cheering section over the years, helped bolster my determination to keep writing as a centerpiece to my career. If I couldn't make it with creative writing or as an independent author, I could still at least keep writing as an asset to whatever I pursued, a tool that would help me advance. And a legal career seemed to fit that bill.

Like an ignorant teenager, I have sometimes become too self-satisfied with my own writing and believed I know everything I need to know about how to perform well. I was once taken down quite a few pegs by one law firm owner. He invoked the writing prowess of the United States Supreme Court justices and

demanded whether I thought I wrote as well as they did. Though this particular attorney often ventured well beyond constructive academic training into the realm of destructive personal attacks, he did have a good point about the justices.

In one recent article, I find one remark by Chief Justice John G. Roberts Jr. regarding the accessibility of law reviews particularly refreshing: "What the academy is doing, as far as I can tell [] is largely of no use or interest to people who actually practice law."[11] As much as I often disagree with Justice Roberts' rulings, he is dead on about this; if I am looking for a law review in research, I have to turn my inner-sifter on full force. At least when you are trolling through case law, you often have the aid of key notes at the beginning of the case that tip you off as to whether the case will help you and direct you quickly to the relevant portion of the case. Or there may be an introductory sentence in the opinion briefly summarizing the facts, issues and outcome of the case. Further still, you may have found the case because it

---

[11] Adam Liptak, Keep the Briefs Brief, Literary Justices Advise, NEW YORK TIMES, May 20, 2011.

was cited by another authority you have already found to be on point, and the citing portion of the new case adds to or provides interesting new dimensions to your argument.

Law reviews are often not written with an eye toward being accessible, but for the writers to crow and preen about their academic superiority, and write in a high brow manner supposedly beyond the comprehension of the rest of the student peasants not fortunate enough to be admitted to the law review. Of course not all law review articles are written in this way; some are crafted with the goal to truly be helpful to the rest of the profession and written in plain English as much as possible. But some law students and lawyers take pride in their legalese and in flaunting it at every opportunity; by doing so they are allegedly more intellectual and beyond reproach in their arguments than those who write in a clear, unambiguous and direct fashion. However, a number of the Supreme Court Justices reveal which style they prefer and themselves practice:

> Justice Ruth Bader Ginsburg, whose writing is clear but dry, said her style

owed something to Vladimir Nabokov, the author of "Lolita."

Justice Anthony M. Kennedy, whose opinions can meander, said he aspired to Ernest Hemingway's stripped-down language, sharing his distaste for adverbs.

Justice Stephen G. Breyer, who has been known to cite foreign law in his opinions, said he looked abroad for literary inspiration, mentioning Montesquieu, Wittgenstein, Stendhal and Proust.

Justice Clarence Thomas said a good brief reminded him of the television show "24."

Perhaps it takes real intellect to be able to convey complex legal arguments in an accessible way, to let the direct words take the audience deeper inside your concepts and see them as you do. Drawing on inspiration from other authors, popular culture, countries and analogies is also a powerful writing tool; it allows the audience to see another facet of your argument like light illuminating another facet of a diamond, another invitation and tour into the world your words create.

In this article, Justice Ginsburg comments on the compulsory urge brief writers feel to use all of the 15,000 word limit allocated to briefs submitted to the

Supreme Court: "Lawyers somehow can't give up the extra space, [] so they fill the brief unnecessarily, not realizing that eye fatigue and even annoyance will be the response they get for writing an overlong brief." In my experience, I have found that if I am using every single word of a brief limit, I am trying to throw everything against the wall and see what sticks, in the classic college style. Using every single word usually indicates a lack of preparedness too; if you have begun your brief early enough you will probably have been pruning and trimming it, going through multiple drafts and having people test-read and proofread it for some time, thereby refining its conciseness and realizing that most of the words you had in the early drafts either did not add to, or detracted from your brief's quality.

I entered Rutgers College as a sophomore, fresh from Mason Gross and a 3.5 GPA. I sought out the Dean of Students to inquire as to the best prelaw major to take. I was advised that I needed to keep my grades where they were and that any major intensive in analytical reading and writing would be wise preparation for law school, as Rutgers did not offer a specific prelaw program. After taking a few courses in Philosophy and Political Science to test them as potential majors, I settled on American Studies, converting my continuing music lessons, activities and credits already earned into a Music Minor.

American Studies seemed to be a perfect fit for me. I had always been interested in popular culture, looking at how people change over time, noting how history often repeats itself, trying to understand certain turning points of different generations, such as Uncle Tom's Cabin and its role in the path to the Civil War, white people's fascination and "slumming" with black culture in the 1920s, the renaissance of the 1960s, all of the social factors that helped make Woodstock what it was, etc. With this major, I would be able to further analyze cultural events and social consciousness, get a reading and writing prelaw training ground, and hopefully benefit from an enjoyable major with good grades.

My focus on grades, in switching to the liberal arts college, proved not to be where perhaps it should have been. In the music school, "A"s were freely handed out largely for just showing up and performing in lasses, lessons and ensembles. It could be that a music student would not have enjoyed such grades if he did not practice, constantly showed up late, didn't make a reasonable effort to study for our few academic requirements, etc. As a music major, I did my work without making it the center of my life. I enjoyed practicing, employing the new techniques demonstrated by my bassoon teacher and experimenting with how my sound could improve according to the quality of reeds I could make. I felt honored to play with the caliber of musicians that came to the school. I played bassoon well but I was not as virtuosic as students who played more competitive instruments, such as saxophone, trumpet, flute or violin. Players of these instruments faced far more competition in any contest, from All-State bands to talent contests to the music school admission process. There is usually a shortage of bassoons in the average music group so I faced far less competition in my musical endeavors. So it was far less difficult for me to obtain a 3.5 GPA than it would have been for me to attain such grades at Rutgers College.

I soon learned what it would take for me to get top grades after switching to a school where most of my required curriculum now consisted of liberal arts classes, and I could no longer pad my GPA with the easy "A"s from performance credits. There was now far less room in the curriculum for credits derived from music. I now had math and science requirements, which had never been my forte. Even the courses which mainly involved reading and writing, which I considered my strengths, required voluminous amounts of studying and reading extremely complex and often cryptic materials on a daily basis, and frequent written assignments which, if prepared correctly, would have required at least ten to fifteen hours dedicated to each project alone. For the math and science subjects which I had particular difficulty in grasping, I most likely should have followed the law school credo of three hours studying for every hour spent in class. What this all boils down to is that I should have spent at least five to six hours studying and doing homework every day, possibly more to maintain or exceed the GPA I had enjoyed at Mason Gross School of the Arts.

I would not ultimately attain such a GPA again until my senior year, when I was further inspired by my fascination of and determination to master speed-reading, my boyfriend boasted an overall 3.6 GPA and I was tired of letting him show me up. By that time it was too late to catch up to him, but my homestretch college sprint boosted me up to 3.2 overall, a respectable GPA for many law schools, albeit not top-tier.

My experimentation with speed-reading arose from my coming across some article or book about this technique, mentioning somewhere that you could speed read by reading books like you would skim through a phone book, as opposing to scanning, which is often confused with skimming. Scanning is when you examine the material in depth, perhaps for passages that are more intricate than others where you need to slow down a bit to comprehend, much like motorists rubber-necking before speeding up again to skimming speed. I found that speed-reading worked reasonably well for short-term purposes, and that I could answer most questions when quizzed by my boyfriend, incredulous that this technique could work.

But it is definitely not the best approach if you want to integrate with literature, come inside the author's world, get to know the characters and have the book stay with you, maybe to the point it changes you or your life.

And speed reading would never work if you want to do well in law school; the material there requires a deep, searching, inquisitive sort of reading, where you ask yourself questions along the way and read the material with different hats on. What would I have done if I was the lawyer preparing this case? What would I have said to prospective jurors during voir dire? How would I have consoled and advised the client? If you were the judge: Could the law have permitted me to reach a different result in this case and if so, how? Did any of the parties' conduct influence my decision? What important precedents did I follow in making the decision?

American Studies in the Law

My chosen major also encouraged a creative look at the law through the eyes of popular culture, and law as seen through television, movies, books and other arts. Some courts even find lawyers' references to popular culture persuasive in argument. Whatever the courts' opinion of popular culture as legal authority, artistic interpretations of the law may also serve as effective learning devices. As I mention elsewhere, learning is often more effective when done hands-on or analogized to something fun. What can examples of popular culture teach us about law or about being better lawyers? A number of movies from the early '90s explore the concept of courtroom justice in memorable, striking ways. Something about this period seemed to arouse our inner sense of pride and social justice and it became increasingly popular to express unpopular opinions out loud, question authority, and take a stand. Events which could have contributed to this:

- The Gulf War;
- The Bosnian War;
- In <u>Texas v. Johnson</u>, the U.S. Supreme Court rules that flag-burning constitutes free speech protected by the First Amendment to the United States Constitution: June 21, 1989;[12]

---

[12] 491 U.S. 397 (1989).

- Nelson Mandela is released after twenty-seven years of imprisonment as punishment for fighting apartheid: February 11, 1990;
- The international grassroots activism of Earth Day: April 22, 1990;
- Passage of the Americans with Disabilities Act: July 26, 1990;
- Attack upon Rodney King by the Los Angeles Police Department: March 3, 1991;
- Announcement by Magic Johnson that he is infected by HIV: November 7, 1991:
- Announcement by Freddie Mercury that he is infected by AIDS and death thereafter: November 22, 1991;
- A federal appellate court reversed the trial court's ruling that the sale of 2 Live Crew's <u>As Nasty As They Wanna Be</u> was illegal and rejected the argument the album should be banned for obscenity, holding that 2 Live Crew's work was an important representation of African-American culture:[13] May 8, 1992;

---

[13] http://en.wikipedia.org/wiki/2_Live_Crew#.22Oh.2C_Pretty_Woman.22_lawsuit.

- Sinéad O'Connor rips up a photo of Pope John Paul II on Saturday Night Live: October 3, 1992.

My Cousin Vinny

This is one of the classic legal drama/comedies of the early '90s, when, in today's parlance, #politicallycorrect was trending. This social phenomenon was accentuated in the contrast between New York City Italians and Deep South law enforcement and small town mores. Almost all lawyers can relate to Vinny's situation in that most of us have been before a judge at some point where we can seem to do no right, and all the chips seem stacked against us. Yet Vinny's common sense, straight-shooting approach also strikes chords with lawyers and the general public alike. We can appreciate slick, street-smart Vinny's refusal to be conned or let anyone pull the wool over his eyes in the context of a criminal case where his cousin and best friend stand accused of a murder they didn't commit: "[The prosecution's] whole case is an illusion, a magic trick. It has to be an illusion, 'cause you're innocent. Nobody - I mean nobody - pulls the wool over the eyes of a Gambini, especially this one."

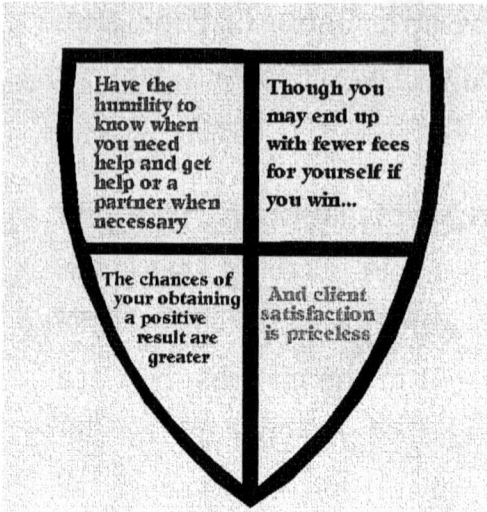

Have the humility to know when you need help and get help or a partner when necessary

Though you may end up with fewer fees for yourself if you win...

The chances of your obtaining a positive result are greater

And client satisfaction is priceless

<u>My   Cousin Vinny</u> also holds an abundance of lessons which, put into practice in real life, can also help attorneys go far:

• Know your local rules of procedure and court rules; these often vary greatly between jurisdictions and can completely change the rules of the game. If you are always used to playing Scrabble where you can use words that appear in any online dictionary and in a new game, you are restricted to words that appear only in one old hardback dictionary, you will be thrown off. Multiply that feeling by the magnitude of appearing in a new court with a plethora of unfamiliar rules, perhaps handling a case with potential severe consequences or the death penalty, as in the movie.

• It is important for success to know your strengths intimately; but also equally important to be equally aware of your weaknesses. Vinny was adept at thinking on his feet, talking fast and not taking any bull, but he was deficient in book smarts and keeping up with information relevant to his case. Vinny's fiancée Mona Lisa fills in the blanks with case preparation and knowledge that he lacks, and one of her skill-sets helps them win the case in a way that no one expected.

- Even in this information age, it could still be difficult to anticipate and avoid some of the sleep-depriving situations Vinny suffered when he had to get to court early the next morning; but do everything you can to get a good night's rest when you have important work to do.

A Few Good Men

When I watched this movie I had not yet been a member of the armed forces; but even though this movie takes place entirely within the context of the military, you don't need to be familiar with military jargon, decorum or etiquette to appreciate the various legal techniques or just plain entertainment value, such as Jack Nicholson's classic smackdown, "You can't handle the truth!" Once again, the problem involves a criminal case, and like <u>My Cousin Vinny</u>, takes place in a culture unfamiliar to most of the audience and to a certain extent, its cast as well. <u>A Few Good Men</u> examines a culture within a culture; a Marine unit perpetually on the border of enemy lines even in peacetime, as an elite subcircle of the military as a whole. As most military and veterans know, there are such elite cadres of armed personnel across all branches of the military. For my own part, I first joined the Army, then later the more exclusive 82d Airborne Division. Within the 82d Airborne there were more exclusive units still, such as the infantry, Golden Knights, and Special Forces. Each of these units share their own unique culture and code, as is true for the subject Marine unit in <u>A Few Good Men</u>.

Amidst the ultra-dramatic themes such as Tom Cruise's reprisal from <u>Top Gun</u> the subplot of living in the shadow of a late great father, we see a number of legal techniques and Lt. Kaffee's straight-shooting dispute resolution, analysis and courtroom approaches:

- Joanne Galloway and Daniel Kaffee stand at opposite ends of the spectrum in the way they practice, which may not be entirely effective for either of them. Galloway tends to overcomplicate disputes, be overzealous and, when she asks her commanding officers to assign her the subject murder case, they privately decide that she is "all passion, no street smarts" and give the case to Kaffee instead. Kaffee congratulates himself on his shoot-from-the-hip ability to bargain his cases into solutions, so much so that he has almost earned a steak knife set from his unit. It becomes clear that Kaffee's classic approach will not work in the case he has been handed, and some kind of medium has to be reached between Galloway and Kaffee's styles of practicing law.

- Listen to your clients; you may be the one to decide the best strategy to get to the goal, but your clients are the ones who determine what the goal is, not you. Kaffee is so wrapped up in his routine of getting plea bargains and getting closer to his steak knife set that at first he does not take his client's wishes seriously. Lance

Corporal Dawson refuses to accept a plea deal in which he would have to plead guilty to involuntary manslaughter and be home in six months because he knows that he would be dishonorably discharged from the Marines if he admits to this crime. For Cpl. Dawson, the Marine code is his life, and he refuses to disrespect that code by admitting he violated it. Cpl. Dawson believes that by following a commanding officer's order to commit a "code red," he upheld the code and served the Corps honorably. Meanwhile, Kaffee wants to take the easy way out and have his client cop a plea because he doesn't believe he can ever prove that the "code red" order was given and doesn't want to lose. Dawson, however, is willing to take that risk, because even if the court decides that he is guilty of murder, he will have still protected his honor and his code. Kaffee must either follow his client's wishes or withdraw from the case, as he almost does.

Philadelphia

This film underscores the fact that American jurisprudence is constantly influenced and changed by the moral views of the public. The film takes place in 1993-era Philadelphia. HIV and AIDS have been emerging as an increasing medical crisis for about the past ten years. These diseases had long been rumored to be the "gay plague."[14] When basketball great Magic Johnson announced he was HIV-positive, many people reacted by questioning Magic's sexuality.[15] Since then, more people have begun to understand that HIV and AIDS do not discriminate between gay or heterosexual, rich or poor, or the color of one's skin. They are still, almost twenty years later, incurable and often fatal diseases that may infect anyone.

Philadelphia also examines the judgment which may befall HIV/AIDS patients according to whether they were at fault for contracting the disease. This judgment becomes a central theme in the movie's employment discrimination trial. As the story opens,

---

[14] http://en.wikipedia.org/wiki/Gay-related_immune_deficiency
[15]
http://sportsillustrated.cnn.com/2009/writers/ian_thomsen/10/22/isiah.magic/index.html

we meet Andrew Beckett, who is a brilliant lawyer who has worked for one of Philadelphia's most prestigious firms since graduating from law school. He is called into a meeting with all of the firm's partners, who announce that he has been appointed lead counsel on an extremely high profile case with an important firm client. During this meeting, one of the partners notices a lesion on Andy's face, which Andy explains away as a racquetball injury.

However, Andy is gay, has suffered from AIDS for some time and has kept this information away from his professional life. Incidentally, a short time after this meeting, when a document in Andy's case is due to be filed at the courthouse to prevent a statute of limitations from expiring, the brief which Andy had meticulously prepared in response to this deadline has mysteriously disappeared. Just before the clock runs out, the firm staff find the brief and get it to the courthouse in time. Nevertheless, Andy is thereafter summoned to a large conference room where all of the partners are waiting for him and the audience already can anticipate what is about to happen.

Joe Miller, the attorney who ultimately represents Andy at trial, initially rejects Andy as a client because of his own personal repulsions about AIDS and homosexuality. However, Joe and Andy eventually run into each other again at the law library. Joe discovers Andy intends to represent himself, and is the midst of reading a Supreme Court case which is central to Andy's imminent causes of action. Joe sits down with him and begins to read from a case which expanded upon the rulings of the U.S. Supreme Court case Nassau Cty. v. Arline, 480 U.S. 273 (1987):

> The Federal Vocational Rehabilitation Act of 1973 prohibits discrimination against otherwise qualified handicapped persons who are able to perform the duties required by their employment... Although the ruling did not address the specific issue of HIV and AIDS discrimination, subsequent decisions have held that AIDS is protected as a handicap under law, not only because of the physical limitations it imposes but because the prejudice surrounding AIDS exacts a social death which precedes the actual physical one...This is the essence of discrimination: Forming opinions about others not based on their individual merits but rather their

membership in a group with assumed characteristics.[16]

This passage is not from <u>Arline</u>, but from some other case, perhaps fictional. Nonetheless it aptly reflects the time and social climate in which <u>Philadelphia</u> was released. The message here seems to not only sum up a central theme of <u>Philadelphia</u>, but also that of the '90s. People began to question more intently why some people did not accept others, as encapsulated so succinctly by Rodney King's "Why can't we all just get along?" Perhaps this question struck such a chord because people were becoming increasingly intolerant of intolerance. I entered college in the fall of 1993, and noticed right away that not only was our student body increasingly diverse, our diversity was largely celebrated and every one of us was celebrated in some way, even myself – a shy, sheltered girl growing up.

Joe then accepts Andy's case and personally serves Andy's erstwhile bosses with summonses. The story then leaps ahead a year to when the case has reached trial, and Joe acknowledges all the themes of the case he and Andy read in the library, including the

---

[16]   http://www.script-o-rama.com/movie_scripts/p/philadelphia-script-transcript-tom-hanks.html

fact that many people hold aversions to gay and HIV/AIDS-infected people.

Joe brazenly forces everyone in the courtroom to question their feelings about gays and AIDS and even concedes that "the behavior of Andrew Beckett's employers may seem reasonable to you. It does to me." But Joe goes on to say that regardless of whether we have a personal repulsion to gays and AIDS, "no matter how you come to judge Charles Wheeler and his partners, in ethical, moral and human terms, the fact of the matter is: When they fired Andrew Beckett because he had AIDS, they broke the law."

In the end, Joe has successfully persuaded the jury to set aside whatever personal aversions they may have to gays and AIDS, causing them to reach a verdict in Andy's favor, awarding $143,000.00 for back pay and loss of benefits and $4,882,000.00 for punitive damages. Though Andy is now on his deathbed, the audience feels a sense of satisfaction that justice has been done.

Andy's fictional case may be compared with the Florida case State v. Casey Anthony, a case which is completely different in many respects. But we may see similarities in the way Ms. Anthony's defense team urged the jury to put aside their personal feelings about the defendant's pattern of lying and partying lifestyle which seemed to come before her daughter and focus on the sole reason the court had convened: to find out what had happened to Caylee Marie Anthony. The defense attorneys acknowledged that Caylee was a sweet, beautiful girl who had left us too soon and the horror that she was gone, just as Joe Miller acknowledges his own personal aversion to gays and AIDS. Yet, the attorneys, both fictional and real, urge the fact-finders that they cannot decide the case based on their own emotions and must follow the law.

Needless to say, the result of the Anthony case is still an extremely emotionally-charged issue, with millions of Americans feeling that justice was not served and a that murderer went free. Others who support the verdict feel that the jurors correctly followed the law and applied the extremely stringent legal standard that "protects an accused against conviction except upon evidence that is sufficient fairly to support a conclusion [] that every element of the crime has been established beyond a reasonable doubt:[17]

> The standard of proof beyond a reasonable doubt…"plays a vital role in the American scheme of criminal procedure," because it operates to give "concrete substance" to the presumption of innocence, to ensure against unjust convictions, and to reduce the risk of factual error in a criminal proceeding. [] At the same time, by impressing upon the factfinder the need to reach a subjective state of near certitude of the guilt of the accused, the standard symbolizes the significance that our society attaches to the criminal sanction and thus to liberty itself. []^[18]

As our well-settled jurisprudence makes clear, "the requirement of proof beyond a reasonable doubt in a criminal case is bottomed on a fundamental value determination of our society that it is far worse to convict an innocent man than to let a guilty man go free."[19] This is not to say that the Anthony jurors necessarily followed the law properly, as arguments can be made that the State proved their case beyond a

---

[17] Jackson v. Virginia, 443 U.S. 307, 313-314 (1979)(page numbers omitted).

[18] Id., citing to In re Winship, 397 U.S. 358 (1970)(page numbers omitted).

[19] In re Winship, 397 U.S. 358, 372 (1970)(Harlan, J., concurring)(page numbers omitted).

reasonable doubt, and that any uncertainty the jurors had was not a reasonable doubt; i.e., "an actual and substantial doubt reasonably arising from the evidence, from the facts or circumstances shown by the evidence, or from the lack of evidence on the part of the State, as distinguished from a doubt arising from mere possibility, from bare imagination, or from fanciful conjecture."[20]

Yet one <u>Anthony</u> juror maintained that the panel wished the law would have permitted them to find Ms. Anthony guilty, but she said that the jurors were "sick to their stomachs" over the verdict and that "..there was not enough evidence. If you cannot prove what the crime was, you cannot determine what the punishment should be."[21] Florida State Attorney Lawson Lamar also conceded that "This is a dry-bones case. Very, very difficult to prove. The delay in recovering little Caylee's remains worked to our considerable disadvantage."[22]

---

[20] <u>Victor v. Nebraska</u>, 511 US 1, 18 (1994), <u>citing to</u> <u>State v. Victor</u>, 457 N. W. 2d 431 (Neb. 1990).
[21] Lizette Alvarez and Bill Carter, <u>Juror in Anthony Case Says Acquittals Took an Emotional Toll</u>, NEW YORK TIMES, July 6, 2011.
[22] Kyle Hightower, <u>Spectacle that was Casey Anthony trial comes to a surprising end</u>, KANSAS CITY STAR, July 5, 2011.

> **If you are a female lawyer, don't let men intimidate you**
> - You will probably experience a lot of sexism in this profession
> - Men at court will assume you are a secretary or court reporter, try to intimidate you
> - Always outprepare them, never let them see all of your cards
> - But if men respect you as a professional, respect them back, extend them professional courtesies
> - Your life as a lawyer will be much easier if you are amicable with your colleagues, male or female

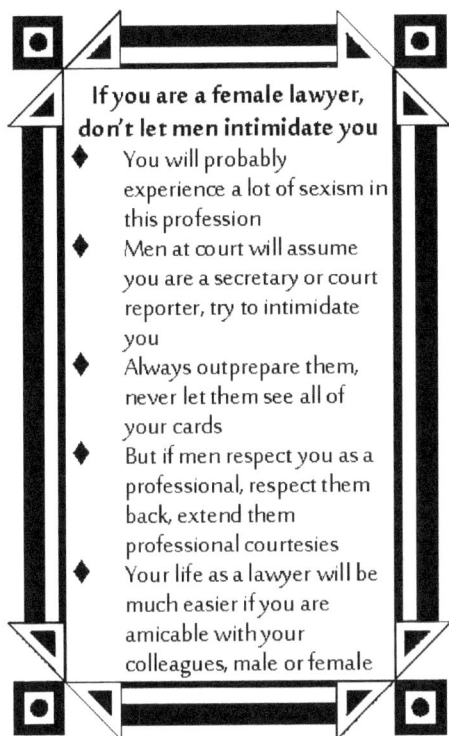

So, even though many Americans did not experience the same feeling of justice served that <u>Philadelphia</u> audiences may have, we still see the application of the same legal principle: asking a jury to set aside their personal feelings or avarice against Andy Beckett (a fictional civil plaintiff) and Casey Anthony (an actual criminal defendant) and follow the law. The bearing which personal feelings and emotions ultimately had on these cases will forever remain unknown, but the *Anthony* verdict underscores the opinion and public policy that an accused is innocent until proven guilty.

Thelma and Louise

This film has become both famous and infamous for its tale of two female desperadoes fleeing the law across the Southwest in the early '90s. The film caused a stir because some thought it condoned lawlessness and violence; perhaps the scrutiny was greater as the protagonists were women. Though both Thelma is married and Louise has a boyfriend, many questioned the women's' sexuality as they were rejecting the men in their lives for each other, and in the final climax of the movie physically demonstrate how strong their love for each other is. The events of the movie raise questions as to if, hypothetically, these women were in a romantic relationship or married, what rights they would have in the law. This question is particularly relevant now as New York has just joined the increasing number of states who now conduct and recognize gay marriages, conferring the rights and protections of marriage upon couples who never enjoyed such rights before.[23]

While I was at Pace, my criminal law class actually studied a scene from Thelma and Louise to help illustrate and provide comparisons to a legal

---

[23] Thomas Kaplan, Sunday's Rush of Happy Couples Becomes Monday's Steady Statewide Procession, NEW YORK TIMES, July 25, 2011.

principle that can serve as a defense to homicide: self-defense or defense of others.

> The right to kill in self-defense or in defense of one's family or habitation rests upon necessity, real or apparent, and the pertinent decisions are to the effect:
>
> 1. That one may kill in defense of himself, or his family, when necessary to prevent death or great bodily harm. (Citing authority.)
>
> 2. That one may kill in defense of himself, or his family, when not actually necessary to prevent death or great bodily harm, if he believes it to be necessary and has a reasonable ground for the belief. (Citing authority.)
>
> 3. That the reasonableness of this belief or apprehension must be judged by the facts and circumstances as they appeared to the party charged at the time of the killing. (Citing authority.)
>
> 4. That the jury and not the party charged, is to determine the reasonableness of the belief or apprehension upon which he acted. (Citing authority.)[24]

Our class watched a scene in the movie where Louise rescues Thelma from an attempted rape, then

---

[24] State v. Fowler, 108 SE 2d 892, 894 (N.C. 1959)

shoots the offender to death. We learn over the course of the movie that Louise's violent rage was aggravated by her own history as a victim of sexual assault. My criminal law professor asked the class what defenses or mitigating circumstances Louise might or might not be entitled to if she were charged with murder.

A student quickly responded that Louise would not be entitled to the right to kill in defense of one's family, discussing how she might have enjoyed this defense if Thelma had been a family member or a spouse. The class then discussed how society often pigeonholes relationships as friendships or fails to even recognize them, when the people involved in these relationships often have as much or more love for each other than if they were related or married. This may have been a criticism many had of Thelma and Louise, as the women's relationship did not fit into a neat or perhaps acceptable category.[25]

---

[25] Often, when two women are particularly close or love each other, modern society sometimes sexualizes their relationship when this may be an inaccurate characterization. For instance, Emily Dickinson wrote intensely affectionate and reverent letters to her sister-in-law Susan Gilbert, which has caused some to speculate that the two had a romantic relationship. Or perhaps these letters represented the love of a friendship between women in the 1800s, when women had far less

We also discussed whether Louise's emotional state could have served as a mitigating circumstance and whether she could have received the defense of acting "in the heat of passion on sudden provocation."[26] The trial court in one Supreme Court case had instructed the jury that "malice aforethought is an essential and indispensable element of the crime of murder," and if this element did not exist then the

---

authority and rights than they do today, and such affection may have been customary in the unique camaraderie they shared:

June 11, 1852
...
I need you more and more, and the great world grows wider, and dear ones fewer and fewer, every day that you stay away -- I miss my biggest heart; my own goes wandering round, and calls for Susie -- Friends are too dear to sunder, Oh they are far too few, and how soon they will go away where you and I cannot find them, don't let us forget these things, for their remembrance now will save us many an anguish when it is too late to love them! Susie, forgive me Darling, for every word I say -- my heart is full of you, none other than you is in my thoughts, yet when I seek to say to you something not for the world, words fail me. If you were here -- and Oh that you were, my Susie, we need not talk at all, our eyes would whisper for us, and your hand fast in mine, we would not ask for language -- I try to bring you nearer, I chase the weeks away till they are quite departed, and fancy you have come, and I am on my way through the green lane to meet you, and my heart goes scampering so, that I have much ado to bring it back again, and learn it to be patient, till that dear Susie comes. Three weeks -- they can't last always, for surely they must go with their little brothers and sisters to their long home in the west!
http://www.sappho.com/letters/e_dickinsn.html
[26] Mullaney v. Wilbur, 421 U.S. 684, 685 (1975).

homicide would be manslaughter under Maine law. The "heat of passion" defense to murder has been defined as "'provocation' sufficient to cause an 'ordinary [person] of average disposition... to act rashly or without due deliberation and reflection, and from this passion rather than from judgment.'"[27]   Since the assailant was attacking Louise's best friend, Louise had to call him off at gunpoint and he began spewing violent, hateful and vulgar remarks her way, perhaps a jury could have found that Louise acted in the heat of passion.

Another defense which invokes one of the central themes of the movie is whether Louise was also suffering from "battered women's syndrome."[28]   A California court has defined battered women's syndrome as "a series of common characteristics that appear in women who are abused physically and [] psychologically over an extended period of time by the dominant male figure in their lives."[29]   The movie eventually reveals that Louise herself was the victim of

---

[27] People v. Breverman, 77 Cal.Rptr.2d 870, 882-883 (1998).
[28] People v. Humphrey, 13 Cal. 4th 1073, 1083 (1996).
[29] Id. at 1083-1084, citing to State v. Kelly, 478 A.2d 364 (N.J. 1984).

sexual assault, but the audience never learns who the assailant was or how long the abuse lasted.

Music

Though my musical studies did not necessarily relate to law and I met very few people in law school who were musicians, all of my life, and especially so during college, music has challenged and released my mind like nothing else. My mom and dad both loved music and made it part of our home and life. My dad, while a professional classical bassoonist, has always been a composer and an improvisationalist. He has now retired from the symphony where he played for over thirty years and now has much more time to dedicate to his composing. My dad often had his friends over while I was growing up to participate in music circles. It was similar in concept to drumming circles, and many of the percussion instruments you would find in such a gathering would be present, but there would also be other instruments such as my dad on his bassoon, someone on our family piano, sometimes a flute player...My mom had also studied the piano in her youth and would frequently be heard playing Joni Mitchell. It was very important to both my mom and dad that I go to a high school with a good music program.

It was thus that I learned to explore creativity through music.   My dad sometimes liked to collaborate; both of us might play the bassoon or I might play the piano, and we would just jam. It was in high school band there that I learned a real passion for the bassoon, an instrument which my dad plays professionally and hoped I would learn too. When I entered as a freshman, I could barely play a scale, but by the end of the summer going into my sophomore year, I was playing the Mozart and numerous Vivaldi bassoon concerti. My brother had begun playing a recording *ad infinitum* around the house of the Vivaldi E minor concerto performed by one of my dad's teachers, Maurice Allard. Mr. Allard's execution of this piece, and others that I discovered, was jubilant beauty, the sometimes wooden tone of the bassoon transformed into golden singing through the voice of the French bassoon.   I could never replicate this goldenness on the German bassoon I had, but I would always try. In this way my bassoon too found its singing voice. In college, I sometimes improvised with friends in dorm rooms on my keyboard, using an organ tone à la the Doors' Ray Manzarek.

Unless you were a jazz student, you did not learn improvisational skills in my music college; we were trained in the classical musical repertoire: Bach, Beethoven, Mozart, Tchaikovsky, etc. Even if you are not trained to improvise, there is still much creativity in playing music. You read the notes on the page and must pay attention to them in ways you do not read text. There are dynamics (changes between loud and soft), tempo (the speed of the music), key changes (an example of this is when a pop or gospel song goes up a level, sounds more exciting and different; this is a sort of key change called a modulation). You must pay attention to and interpret all of these changes in your performance, as well as observe the directions and cues coming from the conductor.

Additionally, you have considerable creative liberty in the sound that comes from your instrument. When I was first starting out, I just barked along like many fledgling bassoonists, but when I heard Maurice Allard for the first time I knew I had to channel that sound in my own playing. When I felt that I was achieving that sound, my mind soared. When I heard the music in a recording I sang along, in the way I tried to sing through my bassoon when I performed the music.

I can't say what the direct connection is between music and law for me, but I do know that without music, my mind would not be where it is now. I feel that my study and love of music has unlocked recesses in my mind I would not have been able to reach otherwise; little fountains of creativity, concepts off the beaten path, where I constantly challenge the status quo. I also learned to read in that particular, exacting way that performing written music requires, and if you read text with a similar analysis, you may gain greater meaning from the words. Certainly, the markings of music are not there such as dynamics, words such as *crescendo, adagio, cantabile,* fermatas, and clefs. But you may examine the words of the author in that way, analyze why he may have used a particular word, why he discusses some topics at greater length than others, where the author seems to show the greatest emotion, etc. Understanding writing in this way may assist you in becoming a better attorney, and having greater empathy for your clients. To love a wide variety of music is also to appreciate humanity and all of our diversity.

Chapter 4: My New Life as a Paralegal

My first paralegal job was in August 1997. I had just made some rounds with legal staffing firms in New York City. Competition is an inherent part of the city, but in temp paralegal work it soon seemed as though there was enough to go around. My crude résumé reflected no legal experience; merely my new degree and some discussion of my college activities. At that time, there was no additional certificate I had to earn to be considered for paralegal work. Before long I found an agency, then named Interim Legal Staffing, and connected with the interviewing recruiters. As it would always be in the staffing world, I learned to keep close tabs on my phone and at the time, my beeper to jump on invitations to new assignments.

As my initial interview wrapped up, Interim told me they had a project starting the next day in Newark, New Jersey and would get back to me soon on the particulars. I was thrilled to hear from them later that day and the next morning, took the PATH train under

Be original, make your own arguments

Don't go into court using the same old form or old argument for the same issue over and over

the Hudson River to arrive in Newark. I then took a bus down to the job site, a plain brick building that blended into the gray streets.

Several other temps from Interim had also shown up for this assignment. We were taken through stark rooms of office and storage space to a long table with a row of workstation computers. Stacks of brown storage boxes also filled the room. I was then introduced to the process known as document coding. We were each given a box of documents to start with, and then advised on how to handle each document.

The first task was to figure out where each document began and ended. Next, the project client explained what fields of information within the document we needed to find, and then enter into the computer for each item. The first field on the list was the date of the document. For people who had never classified any documents like this, much less legal documents, settling on the correct date could be complicated. For example, there could be a date within the body of the document, but there could be a fax header with a different date. For most documents, if I had to choose between two or more dates, I would usually go with the earliest one.

However, if the document had a certificate of service, I soon learned that this was the go-to point for getting the date. A certificate of service is usually a small block of test at the very end of a legal document where the authoring or responsible attorney attests the date that the document was sent to its addressees, then lists of the names and addresses to which the document was sent on such date. This certificate date indicates when the document was finalized into its current form.

Next, we would need to determine the category of document, names of the author and recipient, whether any key pre-specified terms were present in the document and other fields of information. For each field, we would enter the information into the corresponding data block on our computers. Accordingly, users of the program information we were updating could perform searches based upon any of the fields.

It was in this assignment that I discovered my liking to volume work. Though some people took the approach that they did not want to work themselves out of a job, I always figured there would be more work where that came from. I loved the satisfaction of working quickly and accurately. I seemed to be finishing more boxes than anyone else. I loved hearing the praise and appreciation from the supervisors - here I was making it in the legal field! Maybe I would be offered a permanent job.

A few days into the assignment, one of the supervisors pulled me aside. Here it comes, I thought - my first permanent paralegal position! However, the question posed to me was whether I knew anything about computer programming and hacking. Many of my college friends were proficient in these subjects, and I had spent many hours in the computer labs beside them while they explored new frontiers in cyberspace. However, at least for recreation, there was only so much of sitting in front of a screen I could take. I also did not consider myself to have the highly mathematical, analytical mind and patience which seemed necessary to get hooked on computer science. So unfortunately, my answer to the supervisor that day was in the negative and there was no discussion of my coming on as a permanent employee.

I still continued to rip right through my share of the voluminous boxes of documents to which there seemed to be no end. I would quickly get into the rhythm of entering data in the program every morning and I loved the feeling of

Don't overbill your client
- Don't bill for every word and every minute
- Ask yourself, if you were the one to receive the bill, would you think it was reasonable?
- Send your client copies of all the work you do and send them frequent letters updating them on the case so they can see the volume of product you are putting out and how hard you are working

competing with my peers, and winning. I felt sure I had entered the right industry, and was on the road to become a lawyer one day.

The Newark assignment would prove to only last about a week or so for me before I was whisked off to another project by Interim. For my new job site, I joined the crowds along the 4, 5, and 6 subway lines to push onto the bustling morning trains and zoom to uptown Lexington Avenue. There, I would enter the world of the blue-chip New York City law firm of Skadden, Arps, Slate, Meagher & Flom.

A team of other Interim temps were also joining me on the assignment. As a side note, I have always been happier on assignments where I was joined by other temps. There is a different office culture between temporary and permanent staff, who sometimes called us "temps" in a derisive, imperious manner. To some of the permanents, we were like servants called in to wait upon them hand and foot. There is always strength in numbers. You feel less singled out when you're on a team of temps tasked with doing the same thing; you are then able to work with peers with whom you can ask questions and collaborate.

The Skadden project dealt with a large-scale products liability case, and the temps were the ground level of what would be a brand new department of support staff devoted to the case. In 1997, I was just beginning to learn about case management techniques, in the context of a voluminous nationwide litigation.

Our first task was to organize all of the documents and place them in chronological order. We were also tasked with distributing mail and other case documents to the assigned attorneys, and quickly locating and delivering any item they might need.

I soon learned how to create a document index, similar to what I would use in another case years later (see Chapter 12). At this stage in office management technology, the only tool I found to conduct electronic document searches was the word processing search feature. At that time, we used Corel Word Perfect; in years since most office environments have switched to Microsoft Word. As long as the index fields contained sufficient data to yield document search results which would permit the user to locate the item sought by the attorney, this document function was an effective case-management tool. Sometimes however, the attorney would not be able to provide us information about the sought item which corresponded with our index fields, so we would often have to use processes of elimination or deduction.

There was a team of attorneys assigned to this particular litigation as well; one partner, one senior associate and several junior associates. The support staff often made rounds to each of the attorney's offices to deliver mail and any particular needed items. I made the acquaintance of one young associate on the case through these rounds. He resided in a narrow office in a row of many, with a large plate glass window facing another skyscraper dozens of stories up. He usually had Z100 playing on his radio with such tunes as Sugar Ray's "Fly" wafting innocuously into the enclosure.

This young associate was always friendly, mildly humorous and jovial with me; we exchanged routine pleasantries as I made my deliveries and snatched a fleeting view out his window. One day he had a brief conversation with another associate where he asked her for a form, laughing "I'll just put 'deny, deny, deny.'"[30]

---

[30] Of course this tactic is a recurring theme in legal practice, but not always what happens behind the unwritten scenes. I have sat across the desk from many attorneys as they picked up the phone, called opposing counsel, enjoyed a few minutes of introductory jibes and then said "Okay, what are we going to do with this case?" When the conversation takes this turn attorneys may acknowledge weaknesses in each other's cases, knowing that such conversation is off the record, they are not bound to any admissions made therein, and are not prejudiced from making different or contrary allegations in court papers. These same attorneys may put comparatively militant assertions in written

On a few occasions, I entered the office of the partner overseeing the case. It was the epitome of opulence. I felt like looking around too much would be like daring to look at a king so I saw little more than rich, luxurious furniture and a rug. But I was immediately heartened by prospects of a legal career in seeing the heights to which this woman had risen. I spoke to her very little but she was someone sure of her every step; imperious, wise and formidable. I felt like such a timid mouse in her office; could I ever wield that kind of power? I would later learn that every attorney does in fact possess that kind of power but whether or not they use it or even see it is another matter altogether.

The mail and files flowing into our department continued to grow and mushroom. Before long, our team was relocating from our conference room in the middle of corridors, cubicles and offices and down to the lower level of the building, where we would have our own floor. All of the permanent paralegals got

---

filings, but talk to each other like drinking buddies offline. I have observed these sort of conversations more frequently between men; the paternalistic and "good old boys club" nature of law are still quite pervasive, perhaps more so in the south, where I have practiced law thus far.

their own offices and the temps were given that floor's conference room. More permanent staff had joined our team and we even had four case managers, all at different levels of seniority. The second-level case manager was working with some of the perms on a new computerized case management system where we would not simply have to rely on the Word Perfect search features. I never learned many details of this system as it was being developed very shortly prior to the end of our assignment, but it seemed to be more sophisticated than anything I had seen before. There were several computers dedicated to this system in a single room, and only the supervisors and certain staff were privy to the details of this system.

After leaving the products liability assignment, I would go on to numerous others, many of which involved document coding similar to what I had learned in the Newark project. These projects would almost always include other temps, some of whom were graduates from law school and even admitted attorneys who had not found attorney positions yet, even in the healthy economy of the day. I performed several such assignments at Sullivan & Cromwell, an imposing law firm occupying several floors of a skyscraper overlooking Battery Park, adjacent to Wall Street. The interior design featured such spaces as meticulous colonial American, in which carved wooden chairs with floral-patterned cushions and oil paintings of foxhunts resided.

There were more perks here too. The temp team would sit in a large room with windows on two sides, looking out to the adjacent skyscrapers. We had more room now. If there was a lull in the supply of discovery boxes being delivered to us and we ran out of work, we were given a few hours off with pay to go off and do whatever we wanted. If we worked very late, the firm would pay for us to order dinner in - sushi, Italian, sandwiches; the finest New York delivery had to offer. If we wanted dinner before the firm café closed around 8:30, we could also eat there for free. Then, we could have a

> On your resume, talk about all of your experience and jobs in terms of your accomplishments – what are you most proud of from all of your work?

company limousine drive us home after hours too – one girl had the limo drive her all the way back to her apartment on the Rutgers-New Brunswick campus, about thirty-five miles away.

I continued on with these intermittent assignments in the city for the next year and a half. The projects would range anywhere from a few days to a few months. For the most part, they continued to be document coding jobs, but occasionally I was called upon for a receptionist, contract proofreading, or secretary assignment. The work was fairly consistent; I eventually received assignments from three different agencies.

I knew that in entering the legal support staff industry, I would also use the experiences to gauge whether I thought an attorney career would be a good fit for me. Most of the attorneys I was around seemed extremely accomplished; clearly they had secured positions with prominent firms and companies. Some of the attorneys were austere and snobbish, but others, particularly young associates, were often warm and approachable. As I met more and more lawyers, took their directions, journeyed up the elevators to views out to Coney Island and walked the lush, polished hallways, I became further convinced that I would take the next step and become an attorney.

Chapter 5: Pace

In applying to law schools, I had been wait-listed, then accepted at Rutgers School of Law-Newark. U.S. News now ranks Rutgers as 84 and Pace as 117 in law school rankings.[31] I am not sure what the respective rankings were in 1998, when I was poised to enter law school that fall, though I know that Rutgers was still more highly ranked overall. However, my inspiration for becoming a lawyer was environmental law. Pace was then, and is still, ranked third in the country in environmental law, right behind Vermont Law School and Lewis & Clark College (Northwestern).[32] So I left the overall increase in prestige behind for a school that I hoped would eventually launch me into environmental practice full force. I read Pace's promotional materials and was excited about the fact that one of the Kennedys, Robert F. Kennedy, was (and still is) a professor at Pace, co-running the Pace Environmental Litigation Clinic. This clinic then focused on the same objectives as it does now:

---

[31] http://grad-schools.usnews.rankingsandreviews.com/best-graduate-schools/top-law-schools/law-rankings, as of July 11, 2011.
[32] Id.

> The Environmental Litigation Clinic represents public interest environmental groups bringing citizen enforcement actions in state and federal courts on a variety of environmental and land use issues. The major client of the Clinic is the Riverkeeper, Inc. Amicus curiae briefs in significant national environmental litigation are also prepared.[33]

Unfortunately, this clinic was not available to first year students; I would first need to tread through the classes, horn books, and cases which seem to be the bread and butter of the universal 1L curriculum everywhere, such as <u>Pierson v. Post</u>,[34] <u>Burger King Corp v. Rudzewicz</u>,[35] <u>Erie Railroad Co. v. Tompkins</u>,[36] <u>Spivey v. Battaglia</u>,[37] and <u>Wood v. Lucy, Lady Duff-Gordon</u>.[38] If I had to just be a generic law student for one year before really getting into what I came there for, I felt I could live with that – at least at the time.

Anyone planning to attend law school should certainly strive to achieve the best grades possible. Whether or not you want to work in the large,

---

[33]   http://www.pace.edu/school-of-law/centers-and-special-programs/clinics-0/environmental-litigation-clinic/about-clinic

[34] 3 Cai.R. 175 (N.Y.Sup.Ct.1805).

[35] 471 U.S. 462 (1985).

[36] 304 U.S. 64 (1938).

[37] 258 So.2d 815 (Fla. 1972).

[38] 164 NYS 576 (1917).

> **Don't Let People Stack Stuff On Your Desk**
> - This is your personal workspace
> - The only person who should be able to put stuff on your desk is you
> - This give you extra control and autonomy over your work

prestigious firms, more opportunities will open to you based on your academic record. Our reputations as attorneys begin from the first day we walk into law school. It is best to take the process seriously. Law school is not the same as college; there is less room for freedom and trial and error.

Before a student enters law school, she should declutter her life and make way for the full devotion to law school and study. Decide on your study location of choice, whether that be from home or in the library. Buy any necessary books and complete any pre-semester assignments as soon as possible. Pamper yourself and indulge (within reason) in any purchases you think will help you to be a better student – these are worthy investments. These might be school supplies, decorations for a study space, a special pen, a good lamp, study music, a water cooler, a comfortable chair, a new desk, a school wardrobe, etc.

When I entered Pace, I was fully engaged in the academic process and also felt like a bit of an intellectual, since I was there on a substantial scholarship. I commuted to Pace via Metro North, which gave me some extra reading and relaxation time in the morning after rushing through the Manhattan crowds to the train station.

My most valuable study tool proved to be a small adjustable desk lamp which helped me to burn the midnight oil. My study area at the time was a little tapestry-adorned refuge under the platform bed in my East Village apartment. I soon fell into a comfortable study routine. Upon returning home every evening, I would have dinner, work out and unwind a bit, then retreat into my study refuge.

It is often said that you should attack your to-do list in the order of shortest time to complete. This is often a good approach unless you are under a deadline or time crunch to do something else first. By knocking work out quickly, you will get into a rhythm of productivity faster and by the time you get to the longer, more complicated tasks, you will be in such a good work mode that the tasks will seem less daunting and more doable.

Usually, my law school assignments would consistently include reading and briefing cases every night. Each case would usually take about the same amount of time, except for the rare enjoyable case which was a page or less. I would begin by reading quickly through a case, not worrying about whether I understood everything or not, with the goal being just to finish. After the first read-through, if everything wasn't clear I would read the case a second time, slower and more thoroughly. By this point I would know where to locate all four fields of information to go into my brief, IRAC (Issue, Rule of Law, Analysis of Law and Facts, Conclusion).

Sample Briefs

Mohr v. Williams

Supreme Court of Minnesota, 1905

95 Minn. 261, 104 N.W. 12

Parties – P [plaintiff] - patient, D [defendant] - doctor

c/a [cause of action] - battery

Below [procedural history] - jury verdict for $14,322.50

judge denied D's motion for judgment nov, but granted a new trial on ground that damages were excessive

Facts - P went to D, ear specialist, about trouble with her right ear

-       after D examined her, he found a diseased condition in her right ear and she consented to operation on it
-       After P was unconscious under anesthesia, D decided that condition was not serious enough to operate on
-       however, D noticed worse condition in left ear and decided to operate on that
-       operation was skillfully performed and was successful

Issue - If P gave consent for operate on one ear, had she effectively given consent for D to operate on the other ear when it would be beneficial to do so and D did so successfully?

Argument -

D - the act did not amount to an assault and battery

Rule - every person has right to complete immunity of his person from physical interference of others, except insofar as may be necessary under doctrine of privilege

- any unlawful or unauthorized touching of the person of another, unless in the spirit of pleasantry, is an assault and battery

Reasoning [**Analysis**] - Dr. has good faith in operating on his patients, but there is no medical rule granting him free license regarding surgical operations

- but court cannot lay down rule which would unreasonably interfere with a doctor's discretion, such as in an emergency situation

Conclusion - amount of P's recovery (if she recovers at all) has to take into account nature of disease, the benefit incurred and D's good faith

Notes

1. With battery you don't have to take into account whether D meant good or bad.

2. That was an emergency situation and Dr. was entitled to use his discretion, public policy supports this.

3. Case today is still sound law.

Vincent v. Lake Erie Transp. Co.

Supreme Court of Minnesota, 1910

109 Minn. 456, 124 N.W. 221

Parties - P: owner of dock

D: owner of steamship

c/a - damage to property

Below - verdict for Ps

·   from order denying new trial, D appeals

Facts - 11/27/1905 - D's steamship was moored to P's dock to unload cargo

·   at 10pm a storm grew to 50 mph winds

·   D tried to get a tug to tow him from the dock but couldn't get one b/c of the storm

·   the steamship remained moored to the dock and was constantly thrown against the dock, resulting in damages of $500 to P

Issue - was the storm so bad that D did not have a choice in leaving his boat there, no matter whether it would cause damage or not?

Rule - when there is a situation where rules regarding property rights are suspended by forces beyond human control, and there is no direct intervention by D, the property damaged should be held attributable to act of God and not to wrongful act of D

A Rambler's Road To The Law

103

Reasoning - it would have been unwise for
D to take ship away from the dock

·   nothing   more   than   ordinary
prudence and car was expected from him

·   but since owner deliberately held
ship against the dock and he preserved the
boat at the expense of the dock, D should
be responsible for the damage he caused

Ploof v. Putnam - you cannot eject
someone from your property if they have a
public necessity to be there

- but if you are just exercising private
necessity, then you have to pay damages

- you do have the ability to trespass to
protect yourself, but if you do exercising
private necessity, if you can damage as a
result, you have to pay

·   you can take what is necessary to
sustain your property but you will have to
pay for it

Order - affirmed

As shown above, case briefs do not necessarily have to
be lengthy or complicated. The main goal for me was
to synthesize what a case had to say into my own
words, and by writing about it, a reader can fully digest
the message of sometimes extremely complex legal

opinions, sometimes written hundreds of years ago in what seems today like a foreign language.

A good case brief should prepare you for being questioned about it by your professor, in the Socratic method. This bastion of legal training, infamous to most law students, involves a professor selecting a single student from an entire class and essentially deposing her as to her knowledge and analysis of a case or problem. The questioning might involve such inquiries as:

> ➢ Ms. Johnson, what was the case of <u>Vincent v. Lake Erie Transp. Co.</u> about?
> ➢ What was the procedural history of this case?
> ➢ Did the defendant have the right to invade the property rights of the plaintiff?
> ➢ Why was the order imposing an award of damages to the plaintiff affirmed?

Not everyone enjoys intellectual conversations; in fact, I have known many people who are incredibly intelligent but hate to "talk shop" and would much rather talk about sports or the weather than have the kind of conversation one is forced to have while subject to the Socratic Method. Many people do not have these kinds of conversations for fun. However, practicing them on your own before you are actually in the spotlight in front of the entire class will be helpful and also get you talking like an attorney.

Think of the professor in these situations as a future judge who may well one day be asking you questions as hard as these, or harder, about your case, whether from your perspective or your opponent's. You will learn that when you go to hearings that the judge will usually expect you to know your case inside and out, to the degree that a law professor expects you to know a case when discussing it under the Socratic Method. Practice of these conversations can be a valuable study group activity.

Again, my main attraction to Pace was its excellence in environmental law. I learned that our Property professor would offer, to those students who obtained a B+ or higher in his class, to serve as his research assistants and interns to work on actual environmental litigation involving property rights. I was enthralled by this opportunity and was determined to make one of those spots. I was working hard, briefing all of my cases, fully engaged in my classes and knew that if I could earn this honor, in addition to the other opportunities at Pace such as the Environmental Litigation Clinic, I would be fulfilling my passions and doing my utmost to secure myself a career in public-interest environmental law.

Exam time came and I buckled down to my studies, creating outlines based on my copious notes taken in class and poring over them. We did not know in what form we would be tested; whether by essay, short answer or multiple-choice. Yet I felt confident in all of the subject matter to able to perform well on any exam format.

Several of the exams came, some of them open-book, and they called for essay answers. Then, the day of the Property exam came. I entered the room with excitement, certain that I would ace this test; property internship, here I come!

We opened the test booklets and it was multiple choice. I felt a bit thrown, as I had not expected this. I had expected essay, based on the professor's style and the complexity of the issues we discussed; I thought that they would warrant our display of understanding and knowledge by essay so we could attack the problems in that depth.

No, the professor was cleverer than that. He knew, like so many professors, that while you can display more knowledge in an essay, it is also easier to fudge. If you don't know the specific information the professor is looking for, you can throw other information against the wall, perhaps everything else you know about the subject and see what sticks, hoping that it will earn you points, perhaps not as the first-best answer, but maybe as the second, even third, etc. Essays do not employ the absolute all-or-nothing demands that multiple-choice testing does.

So obviously, only the correct answer would do, or we would receive no points. I went through the exam, selecting answers, frequently not being certain that I had selected the best answer, but following one of the multiple-choice tactics that your first answer is most likely the correct one, and that you should not second-guess yourself and change it later. I could see that this exam was meant to weed out those students who really had the most refined, pristine understanding of property law as taught by our professor, to reveal those students who shared the same mental approach and analysis to legal problems as he did.

In retrospect, I learned some important lessons here as well, one of which is: Just as you must know your judge in the real world, you must know your professor. Know how she looks at the law and how she expects her students to do so, which is probably to mirror her own approach. Meet with your professor often to discuss classwork and problems, and not discuss what you're doing right but what you're doing wrong. And if at all possible, know the format in which you will be tested. My experience over a combined three-and-a-half years of law school, between Pace and Nova, is that you are usually told the format of the test beforehand, but not always. Once you know the format of the test, find old copies of tests from that professor, in that same format and test yourself, going over the results with your professor preferably, your study group or another student.

Finally, the day of reckoning came when the Property grades were released, posted in the law school hallway with the grades linked to our exam numbers on a grid. I found my number and tremulously, my eyes followed the line across to the grade. C+. My heart sunk.

During the next session of that professor's office hours, I joined a throng of other students, clamoring to know, just like me, whether their grades could possibly have been mistakes. One by one, we learned that the grades were not mistakes. We had misjudged the exam and the way to study for it. I felt that golden internship tangibly slip from my hands. Another woman whom I sat next to in class later told me she had gotten a B+ in Property and was going to the internship, and the pain inside me twisted again.

After that, I did not feel the same about law school. After the winter break, I struggled to keep my studies at the same driving level they had been the previous semester. I had come out with two As, one B+, a B and that sickening C+. By most accounts, I had done well in my first semester of law school. Yet the loss haunted me day after day, and I slipped deeper into depression.

One day, sudden inspiration hit me. One of my friends with whom I'd temped at Skadden Arps had since moved down to Florida with her boyfriend to be near her parents. She was now attending NSU Law and we had corresponded over email lately, comparing notes about our first year of law school. It was the dead of winter in White Plains that February, and snow coated the ground. I would go escape to the sunshine and forget about my troubles for one week - maybe things would be better when I got back.

Florida was paradise. I had only been there on two high school band trips, three years apart, years before. Now, I basked in the sunshine, the beach, Fort Lauderdale, Miami, driving around with my friend, seeing the sights, feeling even younger and more alive than my twenty-three years.

When I came back, my mind was even further removed from law school. It was still back in Florida, in that golden sunshine, that fountain of youth. So ultimately, that's where I knew I had to be. I withdrew from law school with a 3.2 GPA in the second semester of my first year, rented a U-Haul, and struck out down

I-95 southward, alone, bound for my promised land of Floridita.

In many ways, my dropping out of Pace was an obvious mistake. Sure I had suffered a setback but there were still other opportunities; I might have still made it onto Law Review or Moot Court. I could have redoubled my efforts and studied twice as hard to learn from what happened. In dropping out before my first year was complete, I would not earn any transfer credits towards another law school. Pace was, and is still, ranked third in the country in environmental law. This was the place to realize my passion of becoming an environmental lawyer; where, upon graduation, I could potentially have been faced with an array of career options in which to pursue environmental justice in the public interest.

But it was one of those things where everything in my heart said to leave. In retrospect, I cannot say leaving Pace was truly a mistake; it was merely another stepping stone. Depression also played a part in it too, which is something that many lawyers struggle with. It is something that, if you also struggle with it, you need to seek help. Though many people view mental illness as a weakness, it is a disease that needs treatment like any other - pure and simple. There is no shame in getting help. Incidentally, I did seek help for the depression I felt before I dropped out of law school, but I did not believe that staying there and continuing treatment would really solve my problems. Sometimes, you may be in treatment and know in your heart that you need something different. But continue to seek treatment - whether it is with another doctor, in another area, etc. Obviously I am not a doctor and cannot give you medical advice but it is widely known that many lawyers suffer from alcohol and substance abuse, and these maladies can deteriorate many professional careers. Seek help and use that help to determine the best way to live your life and career.

Chapter 6: Fort Lauderdale Secretary

After landing in South Florida and finding an apartment in record time, I immediately set about getting work. The staffing firm for which I had temped in New York City, Interim, also had offices in Fort Lauderdale, and I had discovered this before embarking on my trip. Yet I was not transferring jobs by any means. I had no specific job prospects waiting for me in Florida, though in that day's economy I always just assumed I would get another job after one ended, because I always did.

I did in fact work for Interim on a few temporary assignments, but they were not in large firm settings with a whole team of paralegals like they had been in New York. It was usually a firm who needed someone to fill in while their secretary was out for a week. I had to get used to being the only temp called in, instead of being part of a temp team.

Looking for better job continuity, I started to circulate my résumé in response to paralegal and secretary job ads. I was called by a firm in downtown

Fort Lauderdale who shared one secretary between two lawyers and needed another secretary. And I was ultimately the one to fit that bill.

Being a legal secretary in a small firm proved to be starkly different than being one of many paralegals in Big Law. The demands are much more immediate and exacting. The attorneys' deadlines are usually your deadlines too. In the large law firms, our job responsibilities were much more limited because whatever we did, there was plenty of it. Hence, our paralegal team was assigned to only one case as managing that case was a full-time job.

In a small law firm, it is rarely any one thing that keeps you busy, but dozens of different demands that arise from minute to minute:

➢ Answering phone calls and taking messages.
➢ Transcribing dictations of letters, pleadings, contracts and other documents.

- Answering questions from people in the office who might come up to my desk at any time.
- Obtaining a file or specific document therefrom upon lawyers' requests.
- Processing mail.
- And other unexpected things which arise constantly which keep you learning on the job.

I quickly learned many lessons from the school of hard knocks, arousing the ire of my supervisors from my lack of experience or street smarts in the ways of lawyers and the consequences of my foibles. For example:

- When you answer the phone, never tell the caller that the lawyer is in the office even if he is, before the lawyer has agreed to take the call. Simply tell the caller you will check to see if he is available first.
- For each and every person who calls, you need to get their name, phone number, what they are calling in reference to, and note the time of call so you can transcribe all of this information into a written message for the lawyer. I was told by some people that the lawyer already had their

number, but procedure compelled me to ask them for it again.

➢ Never volunteer information to the caller about a lawyer's whereabouts, what his schedule is, any internal office information, etc. For example, one of my bosses often liked to spend time on his boat in the morning. One time I let that slip to a caller and then I took considerable heat for conveying the impression the lawyer was a slacker who just liked to goof off and fish.

➢ Before you give a draft of any document back to a lawyer for review, make sure you proofread it thoroughly, or if you feel like you're blind to it and need a second pair of eyes, ask a fellow secretary, paralegal or legal assistant you reasonably trust to proofread it for you. There are certain mistakes you do not want to have a lawyer see if possible such as lack of a spell-check, names or other information left over from an old form which you forgot to change, and misplaced apostrophes such as the popular mistake of "it's" as the possessive tense of "it," instead of the correct "its." Such mistakes can reduce your credibility, perception of your competence and professionalism, and cause an employer to possibly see you as more of a liability than an asset.

> When you receive markups on a document from your lawyer, correcting your work, check off each correction with a red pen after you have incorporated the change in your master document. That way you will be less likely to miss any of the attorney's corrections.

> Don't assume you can just throw away a draft with an attorney's markups and corrections on it after you have incorporated the changes into the master document. Many attorneys will want to compare your most recent draft against the most recent corrections they gave you. You need to give the attorney both documents back when you give them the most recently corrected document, unless he specifies otherwise.

Chapter 7: What The Army Taught Me About Being A Lawyer

One day in early 2000 I was just driving down the road and I heard another one of the Army commercials that I'd heard hundreds of times before. This time though, the commercial stuck a chord in me – it mentioned repayment of student loans. Suddenly the Army seemed like an exciting new way out of the loans I was shouldering from college and what I had borrowed for one year of law school. So the next thing I knew, I was enlisted in the Army and on a plane bound for basic training in Fort Jackson, South Carolina.

In many ways, the Army had nothing to do with a legal education. Learning how to handle, clean, disassemble, reassemble and shoot an M-16, at least literally, has no place in a court room. Many of my drill sergeants mocked those in our number (such as myself who got an automatic E-4 ranking by virtue of my college degree alone) who were "edumacated." The general soldier population does not learn how to research, write essays, and debate intellectual issues.

We talked about things like how to clean a kitchen grill thoroughly, how to pack your rucksack and a parachute if you were Airborne, how to hit the ground after a jump, how to soldier-crawl so low that we would not be hit by bullets flying a foot over our heads...

But there are certain times, when I was in the midst of practice, perhaps in front of a judge, that the Army came back to me full force. The way that I sometimes address judges as "Sir" instead of "Your Honor." The posture I had before judges was borrowed from my days of standing at attention. The way that I sometimes starched and ironed my own suits the way I did with my BDUs, instead of always having them done at the cleaners.

The Army is certainly a place where you learn the true meaning of decorum, respect and attention to detail. But these are not the only ways I relate the Army to law school and lawyering.

In the Army, it could often seem like not everyone had your back. There were certain soldiers who rubbed each other the wrong way. I never went

into combat with my fellow soldiers but we did go into
life threatening situations such as parachute jumps. It
did not happen that often, but occasionally soldiers
would die or be seriously injured during jumps.

Have an
open-door policy
and welcome
people to come ask
you questions

In the food service industry,
they say that customers are
never an interruption to your
job, they are the reason for
your job.

It's the same way with helping
people around you, answering
their questions, covering their
hearings for them, helping
each other out.

So there was a certain bond between all of us,
especially the enlisted, male and female soldiers alike.
Drill sergeants were often pure tough love. Most of the
drill sergeants treated us all like their kids, who they
often had to punish, but like kids that they were trying
to protect and teach us how to protect ourselves. The
drill sergeants were constantly emphasizing to us that
what we were learning could mean the difference
between life and death. One time, a drill sergeant told
a soldier to write a letter to her mother outlining how

she had died that day because she had failed to follow instructions. The soldier was then ordered to read that letter to several squads.

This undying and vigilant concern and care for soldiers by our NCOs (non-commissioned officers) stands in sharp contrast to the concern law schools have for their trainees today, and even when I reentered law school in 2001, less than a month before September 11. I never had a professor who told his students to write a practice letter to the Florida Bar to rebut allegations (maybe true, maybe false) where one of our clients had lodged a complaint against us. We never were asked to practice being called before a judge to answer an order to show cause why we should not be held in contempt of court. We never role-played being faced with a vindictive opposing counsel whose only goal was to lie about us, damage our reputation and win his case at any cost. We were never given a sample client trust account to manage and properly account to the Florida Bar in response to an audit. If law school trained in the Army style, it would probably train law students for the worst possible scenarios lawyers can and often do face, such as these.

Not only that, many law schools would follow a business model which was more consonant with the best interests of their students, instead of their current model of gouging tuition, stretching class sizes to the limit, and sugarcoating job prospects, by which from "1989 to 2009, when college tuition rose by 71 percent, law school tuition shot up 317 percent."[39] A New York Times article discusses how some who benefit from the current law school structure, such as deans and law professors, lament the harm the structure causes to its student consumers. Yet these agents of the law school business model say one thing and do completely another, thereby perpetuating the system they denounce so vehemently. As one law professor notes, "My salary [] is paid by the current structure, which is in many ways deceptive and unjust to a point that verges on fraud. But as a law professor, I understand that what is good for me is that the structure stay the way it is."

---

[39] David Segal, Law School Economics: Ka-Ching!, NEW YORK TIMES, June 16, 2011.

Chapter 8:   Return to Law School

In August 2001, as I entered law school once again, I found myself disappointed with my surroundings. For one thing, the first time I went to the law library, I discovered that the library had extremely limited hours compared with my past schools. I had always valued the option to go study late at night, early in the morning or whenever suited my purpose.

Additionally, I was now required to purchase a laptop computer as part of my entrance into the law school. In retrospect, I think this was more for the benefit of Dell, the vendor, than the students, as we were each charged about $2,500.00 for these products. There was no task we had to perform in law school which necessitated this compulsory burden upon the captive student consumers. At Rutgers, the students had access to computer labs where they could log on to public PCs, complete documents, use the nascent Internet and use these public computers as a resource in completing their schoolwork. Rutgers is a public state university, and its tuition was far more modest than that of a private school as NSU is, yet Rutgers tuition included computer and Internet access.

By the time I returned to law school, I just wanted to get it over with so that I could take the bar exam and become an attorney. There are times I regret not having worked harder at NSU so that I may have been admitted into the blue chip summer associate programs, and a permanent position from there. Rather, I have had a hodge-podge of career experiences in different settings, and the approach, prowess, and ethical levels of multiple attorneys. Whether I agreed with them or not, I have forever taken a piece of each of their teachings, much like a conglomerate rock.

With the requirement of a law school laptop purchase came an automatic student email account via the Outlook which came installed with our Windows operating system. This was perhaps the worst distraction of all, perhaps intended to be so by the administration so as to weed out those students who could overcome such temptations. Every day, distractions would rise most conspicuously in the form of ASEs (All-Student Emails). Every so often, an ASE might contain an important announcement or pertinent information which would assist in our studies. But more often than not, ASEs became a shameless forum for chain emails, jokes (ranging from tasteful to frat-house humor) and an endless platform for pontification, verbal jousting, insults and sometimes no-holds-barred wars of words.

Had I known before re-entering law school what the perils of subscribing to the ASE drama would be, I would most likely have stuffed my laptop in the back of my closet. A number of students did quite well sticking to the tools of learning which had served me so well at Pace – a pen and notebook. Certainly there would sometimes be important announcements over email but they would usually be duplicative of what we had been instructed in class or what was readily obtainable from other students.

Some students prefer to take notes in class by typing, can study more efficiently by doing so and can easily synthesize their notes into other study aides, such as outlines and flashcards. However, if you are going to use your computer in class, disable your access to the internet or leave your wireless card at home, and promise yourself that you will not enter the internet during class unless directed to do so by your law professor. You will thus eliminate a front line of detractors to your studies and career right then and there.

At Nova, I also experienced a cliquishness and high-school mentality which I had gratefully found to be in absence at Rutgers. My undergraduate school had been home to over 50,000 students at its New Brunswick, New Jersey campus alone and there was a strong sense of pride, inclusiveness and diversity amongst the student body. I had been painfully shy and withdrawn during high school, but from my first moments at Rutgers I forged real connections and knew I was in the right place. There were student groups and communities for everyone, and there would always be someone who came along to include you and make sure you weren't left out.

I found myself at the opposite end of the spectrum when I entered Nova. The cliques and designations of who was popular or not were formed quickly. Nasty gossip circulated about students and teachers alike. A Darwinist culture was in pervasive existence. It wasn't to the point that I would go to the library looking for a book and find it with pages cut out as some of the law school urban legends went, but it seemed clear that many students only wanted to be friendly and accepting of only certain people. I had just come from the Army, with a culture where, whether you liked everyone or not, you felt like you were a part of a family and you were all working together. The new polarizing environment of NSU was jarring to me. I was not able to gain acceptance to a study group. I sent out an early ASE in an attempt to find fellow musicians amongst the student body with whom to have some steam-releasing jam sessions and only one person, a piano player, responded. I was grateful for the response, but our appreciation of music seemed so isolated amongst our peers, who almost uniformly spent their down time getting smashed.

One of my main draws to law school was the prospect of one day being able to work in public-interest environmental law field, along the lines of Greenpeace and Earth Justice. When I discovered that there was an environmental law society at Nova I was initially thrilled, as I thought this group would consist of other students who had a real passion for the environment, had serious aspirations to one day work in this field, could help each other find opportunities and prepare for same, wanted to get the rest of the law school community involved in learning about environmental law and would organize events where we could roll up our sleeves and make a difference, whether that be cleaning a natural habitat on a regular basis, perhaps attending important environmental court proceedings, and getting involved in our community to hopefully shape local policy for the better.

For the most part, it turned out that the other members of the environmental law society (ELS) were not interested in the above prospects to the extent that I was. There was a beach clean-up project early in the semester, but it seemed like a token good deed for the year after which we could just kick back and engage in primarily self-indulgent recreational excursions. The centerpieces of the ELS's agenda for the remainder of the year included an airboat ride into the west Broward County portion of the Everglades, and an overnight canoeing   excursion   through   the   southwestern

Everglades to an island eleven miles from shore, in the Gulf of Mexico. I attended these events and certainly found our surroundings and wildlife beautiful. The group's tacit intention seemed to be that if they created opportunities for people to visit these places, people would indirectly gain a greater appreciation for the environment. However, if you just wanted to go out there, get blasted and think about no one but yourself, than that was cool too.

I thought it a shame that law school was not strengthening my career goals as undergraduate school had done. I just began to look at it much as I had at high school, predominantly just something to endure. A lesson that can perhaps be drawn from my law school experience on my second go-around is that a student should do some reconnaissance on the social environment of their law school prospects. Obviously getting along with people is important in any context, and in law school you are building your professional reputation, making professional contacts   and possibly finding future business partners. You should find a school where you do not feel alienated or ostracized in the student body, but feel at ease. This may be more and more difficult today as the number of students entering law school increases as much as the available jobs decrease, and competition may be more hostile. But no matter how you slice it, you are stuck with your classmates for the next three years or so and you are each other's captive audience, friends or foes. Find a school where the social environment will work for you, rather than against you, in this 👍- centric society.

Chapter 9: Summer Internship

In the summer between my first and second years of law school, I took a pro bono internship with the criminal division of one of the local trial courts. Some of my colleagues had a derisive attitude toward pro bono work and saw it as a sign as an inferior, less-than-prestigious contribution to a legal career. I was not thrilled about the fact that my only compensation for a full time job would be reimbursement for train fare. Yet, I recognized that the opportunity to work behind the scenes at a courthouse, interacting face-to-face with judges and preparing documents which would be signed into official orders and law was invaluable, regardless of whether there was pay or not. Also, I had lived in New York City, had some introduction to the world of plays, theaters and actors and was aware that quite often actors would take a non-paying part to build up their résumé and hold their own against the fierce competition of the city. If it could pay off for them, it could for me.

I noticed the court advertisement for summer interns through the law school career development office. I called the contact attorney and she indicated that the court was basically taking any applicant who wanted the internship, as there was an extreme backlog of work. The assignment would involve assisting the judges in the circuit criminal division of the court, who were inundated with mostly *pro se* post-conviction motions for relief pursuant to Florida Rules of Criminal Procedure 3.800 and 3.850. The movants were mostly incarcerated and were challenging all or part of the proceedings that had led to their sentence and the sentence itself. They raised such defenses as ineffective assistance of counsel, improper calculation of sentence or crediting of gain time, discovery of new evidence, mistake and others.

On my first day, I took the Tri-Rail up from the Fort Lauderdale Airport Station up to West Palm Beach, and caught a free shuttle from the station down to the courthouse. There was another intern starting the same day as I, and we met with our immediate supervisor, a staff attorney in the circuit criminal division. We looked around her office and saw our work cut out for us; the perimeter of her room was lined with files, presumably in the order of urgency.

We began by each taking a court file; most of the papers indicating the procedural history of the case would be in the file, but the document with which we were primarily concerned was the motion for post-conviction relief. We would then parse through the motions, almost always authored by a pro se defendant, and try to piece together the haphazard arguments usually resulting from arguments latched on to cases that were inapposite to the particular circumstances. We would then conduct research in support of memorandum orders to be drafted for the presiding judge's signature.

An argument I frequently encountered from the movants was the ineffective assistance of counsel claim, for which the movants usually failed their burden to establish. The Supreme Court of the United States has thoroughly discussed the concept of effective assistance of counsel, as part of a defendant's Sixth Amendment right to counsel and what can cause that assistance of counsel to become ineffective.[40] In order to prove ineffective assistance of counsel, a defendant must show that "counsel's conduct so

---

[40] Strickland v. Washington, 466 U.S. 668 (1984).

undermined the proper functioning of the adversarial process that the trial cannot be relied on as having produced a just result."[41]:

> A convicted defendant's claim that counsel's assistance was so defective as to require reversal of a conviction or death sentence has two components. First, the defendant must show that counsel's performance was deficient. This requires showing that counsel made errors so serious that counsel was not functioning as the "counsel" guaranteed the defendant by the Sixth Amendment. Second, the defendant must show that the deficient performance prejudiced the defense. This requires showing that counsel's errors were so serious as to deprive the defendant of a fair trial, a trial whose result is reliable. Unless a defendant makes both showings, it cannot be said that the conviction or death sentence resulted from a breakdown in the adversary process that renders the result unreliable.[42]

The Court emphasized that deference must be given to defense counsel's decisions, and that "every effort be made to eliminate the distorting effects of hindsight, to reconstruct the circumstances of counsel's

---

[41] Id. at 686.
[42] Id. at 687.

challenged conduct, and to evaluate the conduct from counsel's perspective at the time."[43] All attorneys must often think and act on their feet, and particularly in criminal defense law, those split-second decisions can gravely affect a person's liberty or even life. The upshot of <u>Strickland</u> is that if a lawyer is diligently representing a client accused of a crime, she may make mistakes, but unless those mistakes are so severe that the defendant is essentially deprived of

> Before You Go To A Hearing, Try to Have a Mock Hearing With Two Colleagues, One Acting as Opposing Counsel and The Other Acting As Judge

---

[43] <u>Id.</u> at 689.

counsel in the eyes of the law, and those severe mistakes prejudice the client's defense, the lawyer has provided effective assistance of counsel. Therefore, I would usually find the post-conviction claims of ineffective assistance of counsel to be insufficient.[44]

After I had drafted a proposed memorandum order, I would then take the file and order to the judge assigned to the case for review and signature. This process gave me a valuable behind-the-scenes look at what judges do and what can influence their rulings.

The summer staff were also fortunate to be treated to lunch with the judges on a few occasions, where the judges would share valuable insights into what they expected from attorneys appearing before

---

[44] Keep in mind that in any case, whether at state court or the appellate level, a judge may have a staff attorney or legal intern research and prepare her memorandum orders, such that it is really the judge's staff who decides the case. This may occur when, during a hearing, a judge states that she will take the motion(s) under advisement and issue a ruling at a later date. Sometimes you may be able to learn whether the judge has such staff; this will commonly be the case at the federal level. If a judge has taken a matter under advisement, you may be well-advised to quickly obtain some law which supports your side of the case, and transmit it to the judge's office as soon as possible. You might mention in a cover letter that your submission is designed to assist whomever may be assisting the judge in the preparation of the order, so that your research has a better chance of getting to the right person. And as always, when communicating with the judge, be sure to copy opposing counsel; they will probably want to submit law of their own. Also keep this in mind when conducting your research.

them. For example, one judge said that watching good attorneys advocate before them is like watching a play. Sense of timing, self-assurance, persuasiveness, choice of words – such talents are what can draw judges in. These skills often take many years of experience to develop as you cannot completely learn these things just from reading books. But you can give yourself a head-start by knowing your case inside and out, and judges even expect this of you. When attorneys appear before a judge and do not know their case, they lose credibility with the judge, they are tuned out and the judge does not take them seriously.

Judges also commented on how attorneys dress, and some important dos and don'ts. For example, attorneys should take the greatest care to make sure their attire is clean, neatly-pressed, and in good taste. Even the smallest stain or tear in clothing can tarnish an attorney's professional image. Certainly, what is in good taste is open to much debate, but I never felt I could go wrong with a simple black, skirted suit with a hemline no more than two inches above my knees. Some judges do not approve of women wearing pantsuits, so it is best to wear a good jacket, skirt, blouse, pantyhose and dress heels to be on the safe side if you are a woman.

Not wearing pantyhose detracts from a suit's professional appearance and adds an undesirable casual element, as do open-toed shoes or sandals in court. Certainly, not all judges have a problem with a more casual look, but again, be on the safe side. You can hardly ever go wrong with looking your professional best in court.

From living in the South, I have learned that many Southern women are very meticulous and detail-oriented about every aspect of their appearance. They often have their eye-shadow, lipstick and nail polish carefully coordinated with the color of their suit and jewelry. The experimentation with color that many women make can be tastefully done within the boundaries and decorum of courtroom attire. For certain occasions, it is best to stick with basic black but for other, perhaps less dispositive or solemn court proceedings, solid unobtrusive tones, not garish or brash, can add welcome variety.

Just from what I have observed, the most professional-looking men wear good black suits with a white or mildly-colored shirt, a tie and highly-polished black dress shoes. It seems that many men spit-shine their shoes the way I was taught in the Army, using Kiwi or some kind of shoe polish. In the Army, some drill sergeants expected to be able to see their faces in our boots; it is certainly a sharp look when it is achieved and I have seen it in many shoes walking the courthouse halls. Some women's shoes can be polished, but some not because they have a cloth exterior. It can be extremely difficult to keep women's dress shoes looking spic and span as they get smudged and streaked from rubbing against each other or other things, they can start to get little tears and stains on the cloth. It's a good idea to clean and polish, if possible, your dress shoes immediately before and after going to court, and perhaps even every day if you really want to take your work image up a notch. Killer shoes can really make all the difference.

I also learned from working with and for judges that they are people, just like everyone else. Most of the judges were extremely friendly and laid-back behind the scenes, and I enjoyed talking to them about my career goals. I was fortunate enough to obtain a positive letter of recommendation for one of the circuit criminal judges. In the letter, he stated that my work was of a uniform high quality and that he rarely ever had to make corrections to my work, and very minor ones at that.

One judge suggested that to get used to public speaking, I should join Toastmasters. This judge stated that he had been a member of Toastmasters for years and that this group really helps you practice speaking in front of people, holding their attention, and making compelling arguments. When I spoke with this judge back in 2002, I don't know if Toastmasters has a website but they do now, which helps you find chapters near you or teaches you how to start a chapter if there is not one near you already.[45] According to the website,

> There is no instructor in a Toastmasters meeting. Instead, members evaluate one another's presentations. This feedback process is a key part of the program's success. Meeting participants also give

---

[45] http://www.toastmasters.org/

> impromptu talks on assigned topics, conduct meetings and develop skills related to timekeeping, grammar and parliamentary procedure.

After all, it is much better to practice out loud, in front of strangers where you will feel jitters but everyone is in the same boat, than to go cold into court without the benefit of such experiences, there is no more chance for practice and it is already game time.

Chapter 10: Inside a Solo Practice

————————————————

In the summer before my third year of law school, I began working for a solo practitioner, Mr. Hugh.[46]   Mr. Hugh had been practicing law for over thirty years and he was winding down his practice. He was looking for a paralegal to assist with what proved to be the last involved litigation matter he would take. When I interviewed for Mr. Hugh, he told me that he was having the applicants write a memorandum of law to resolve a question pertaining to a generalized set of facts, which I found later to relate to his actual litigation case. I prepared the test memo the evening after my interview and returned it to Mr. Hugh promptly via email. Perhaps because I was the fastest candidate to complete the interview challenge, Mr. Hugh selected me as his new paralegal.

We quickly got down to business. Though I only worked for Mr. Hugh for about fifteen to twenty hours per week, which schedule continued for approximately the next two years, my time with him involved rigorous

——————————————

[46] Name has been changed.

training. Mr. Hugh was extremely thorough and meticulous as we worked through each assignment. He was a man of unwavering conviction and confidence in his own thoughts and arguments. In my initial interview, Mr. Hugh told me he had not lost even so much as a motion in five years. I would only see him lose one motion in two years; an opposition to a motion to amend complaint, when such opposition is usually fruitless. However Mr. Hough decided to oppose the amended complaint because it now included a claim for nominal damages, and the parties were engaged in a contractual dispute. The upshot of this was that if our opponent was awarded even so much as a dollar in nominal damages, he could be entitled to recoupment of his substantial attorney's fees from our client, as the contract provided that attorney's fees would go to the prevailing party. And of course, even an

Don't sell yourself short on fees

☆ Don't let people con you into working for free

☆ Before you even meet with a prospective client and ask them for money, find out if they are serious, respect you as a professional and are prepared to pay you accordingly

☆ Determine before you take a client on whether they are just trying to get free advice out of you, if so, you will probably always have payment problems with them

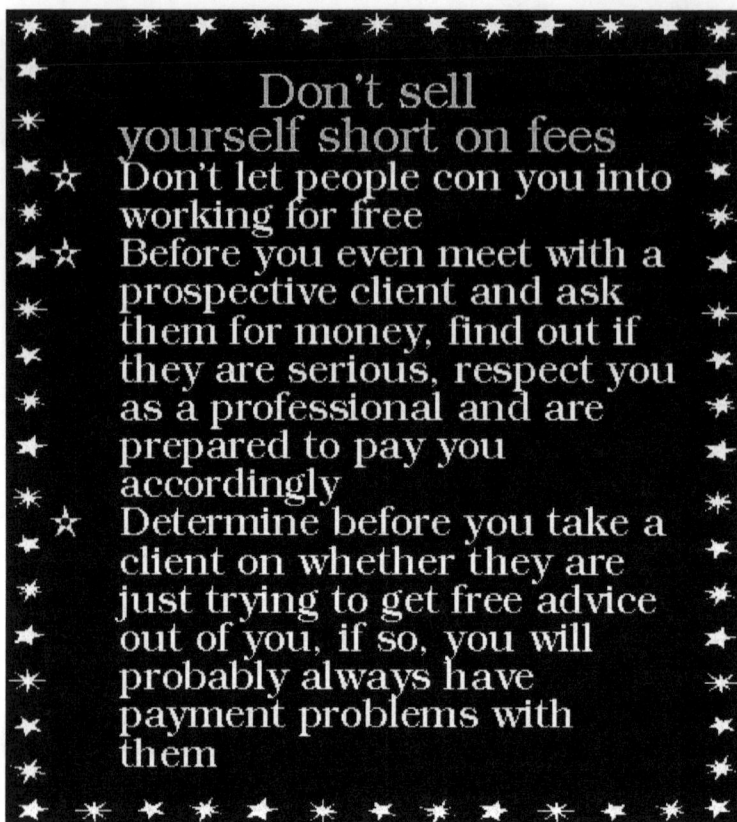

award of nominal damages can establish someone as the prevailing party.[47]

Right away, Mr. Hugh and I worked on drafting motions and the underlying research. Mr. Hugh would sit authoritatively behind his desk and tell me his view of the facts, and then ask me to research a particular issue to find law to support our position. Mr. Hugh

---

[47] Farrar v. Hobby, 506 U.S. 103 (1992).

subscribed to Loislaw, a more economical legal research resource than Westlaw or Lexis, though its search parameters are much more limited. Even so, I was usually able to quickly find a number of statutes or cases which would contribute to Mr. Hugh's arguments.

I would then proceed to draft legal memoranda embodying these arguments, and Mr. Hugh missed nothing in reviewing my work; removing immaterial commas, incorrect pronouns left over from the previous document template, pruning garrulous sentences, and questioning me as to what I meant when my word choices missed the mark. We would go through no less than three drafts of everything, usually more. Mr. Hugh always had me work on a document well in advance of the deadline or when he planned to submit it. Often he would decide to delete significant portions of previous drafts in his refinement process.

Our primary case dealt with a property owner who had rented commercial space to a tenant who, according to our owner client, abandoned the property and the lease, justifying our client to re-let the property to another tenant. The first tenant then came back claiming he had never abandoned the property and launched a multi-count lawsuit against our client based on numerous theories of tort.

Mr. Hugh then directed me to draft a motion to dismiss the complaint. At that point, I knew very little about what that entailed; through research I discerned that each cause of action required that certain allegations, or elements of the claim be stated by the plaintiff. I started by going through the complaint and making a list of each cause of action alleged, which included breach of contract, tortious interference with a business relationship, fraudulent inducement, conspiracy, conversion, and specific performance. If all elements of a cause of action were not presented, a basis to dismiss that particular count existed.

Never Go to A Hearing Without An Order Drafted the Way You Would Like A Judge to Rule

Every aspect of Mr. Hugh's practice was meticulously managed and maintained. I have forever followed Mr. Hugh's example in his template for a caseload list. First, I would create a landscape-oriented document, then insert a table with three columns such as the following:

Rebecca's Caseload List

as of Sunday, September 4, 2011

Sally Client 510 S.E. XXX Avenue Anytown, Florida 330** Home: 954-XXX-XXXX Cell: 954-XXX-XXXX Sally's Summer Residence 5555 S. ******* Blvd. Anytown, NY 100** 212-XXX-XXXX	Evidentiary hearings: 2/7-2/8, 10-12 & 2-4 each day Get subpoena out by 1/11 Begin preparing motion for summary judgment Receive worksheet from Sally by no later than Wednesday, 1/4	Counsel for Opposition: Robert ********, Esq. P.O. Box 130 Anytown, Florida 33*** 954-XXX-XXXX Fax: 954-XXX-XXXX Clerk of the Court Room 252 Honorable ****** Room *** (954) 831-XXXX Fax: (954) 831-XXXX Broward County Courthouse 201 S.E. 6th Street Fort Lauderdale, Florida 33301
Wife v. Husband Office: 954-XXX-XXXX Fax: 954-XXX-XXXX	She needs faxed to her a new financial affidavit	Counsel for Husband Joann *******, Esq. P.O. Box 1234

emailaddress@anydomain.com	form and the copy of the original fin affidavit from '99.	Anytown, Florida 33***-1234 emailaddress@anydomain.com
954-XXX-XXXX (Client's private office line)		Judge ************* 545 1st Ave N, Ste **** Saint Petersburg, Florida 33701-3705 Phone: 727-XXX-XXXX Fax: 727-XXX-XXXX

The landscape orientation helps to give you more space to type in each column. In this format, in the first column we have contact information and other important general information pertaining to our client. In the middle column, we put all outstanding tasks, due dates, and any other assignment or event to be completed. In the third column, we put contact information for all opposing counsel, any judge or court information, or other third party contacts.

Over the years, even with the advent of Outlook, Amicus, Pro Doc and other case management platforms, I still like this caseload format. Mr. Hugh would always carry a copy with him and a copy printed out in the office. Often, the fields in other programs like Outlook often give you a limited space to put information, sometimes it will be cut off or be too small to be legible in a print out. Other times, you would have to generate several different reports to obtain all the information about your cases you want to have handy at any given time. In Mr. Hugh's format, you can constantly customize the information you want at your fingertips about your cases and not have to worry about the limitations of program fields.

Chapter 11: Study for the Bar

I took a hiatus from working with Mr. Hugh while I launched into study for the Florida Bar Exam. Though I may not have fully applied myself during law school, I determined that I would make up for past mistakes in my approach to bar study. My last law school exam was over with sometime in early May that year and I remember that many students were knocking off for a few weeks to vacation and party before graduation and buckling down to study. Some students also had a job and decided to keep working while studying for the bar. The job market was tough, but nothing like it is now and more to the point, I saw no point in jeopardizing admittance to the Bar and exclusion from attorney work in favor maintaining a legal staff or career field other than what we had all spent years and tens of thousands of dollars to obtain.

I signed up for both BarBri and PMBR. Some students felt that signing up for BarBri, the study program that focused on the state portion of the exam, alone would be sufficient preparation. However, the multistate-focused PMBR offered books of sample questions and tests whose problems were widely accepted to be commensurate in difficulty to the actual questions on the bar exam. PMBR claimed in advertisements that the passage rate of students who supplemented their state studies with the multistate program was much higher than those who did not. This claim made sense to me, because I did not think I would be able to pass the bar exam without constantly taking practice tests as close to the actual level of difficulty as possible. I knew just listening to lectures would not be enough.

So I immediately set down to study and try to digest a universe of information. The goal for me was not to retain any of the information long term. This was simply like one big brain teaser; a game that needed to be won and I had to learn the rules of the game.

I soon realized that the most important thing for the state portion of the exam would be to memorize as much information as possible. The state portion would involve question/answer and essay problems and by memorizing information, I would be more likely to independently provide the correct information without the benefit of having my memory jogs by multiple choice suggestions. I soon turned to the best memorizing devices I have ever used: flashcards.

I took my state bar exam books, sat down to my scanner and just started scanning for hours, until I had scanned in all of the pages with information which could possibly be on the test. Once this was done, I began formatting each unit of information into flashcards. What a unit of information might be depended on the scope of the issue. For example, if I wanted to have a flashcard about Florida Rule of Civil Procedure 1.140, I would simply put the name of the rule "Defenses: When Presented" on one side of the flashcard and present of the substantive issues that pertain to that subsection. We were not required to know the numbers of any rules, statutes or other laws on the bar exam, so I would simply classify my flashcards according to issues denoted in the laws. Of course there are always exceptions to the rules, but in summarizing a rule I would state what is generally the case, and deal with any important exceptions in a separate flashcard.

Defenses When Presented

- A defendant shall answer a complaint, cross claim or counterclaim within 20 days of service

- An answer to an amended pleading is due within 10 days of service

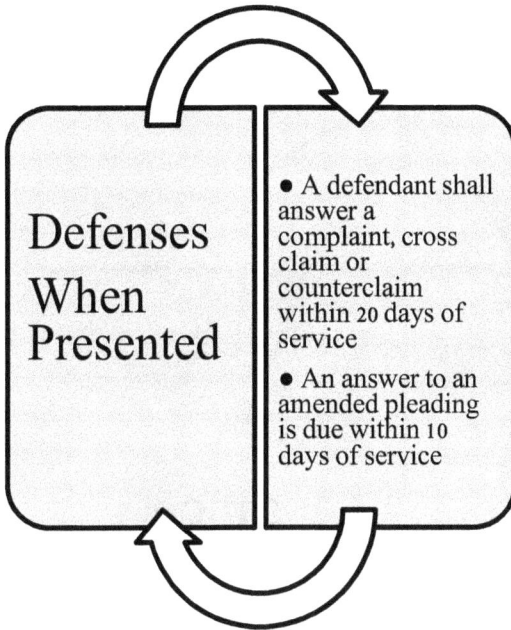

For elements of a cause of action or any list of factors included in any legal principle, I would create an acronym and think of a phrase by which I could remember the acronym. If I could remember a phrase which would jog my memory as to the letters of an acronym, I would probably be able to remember the underlying principles for each letter of the acronym.

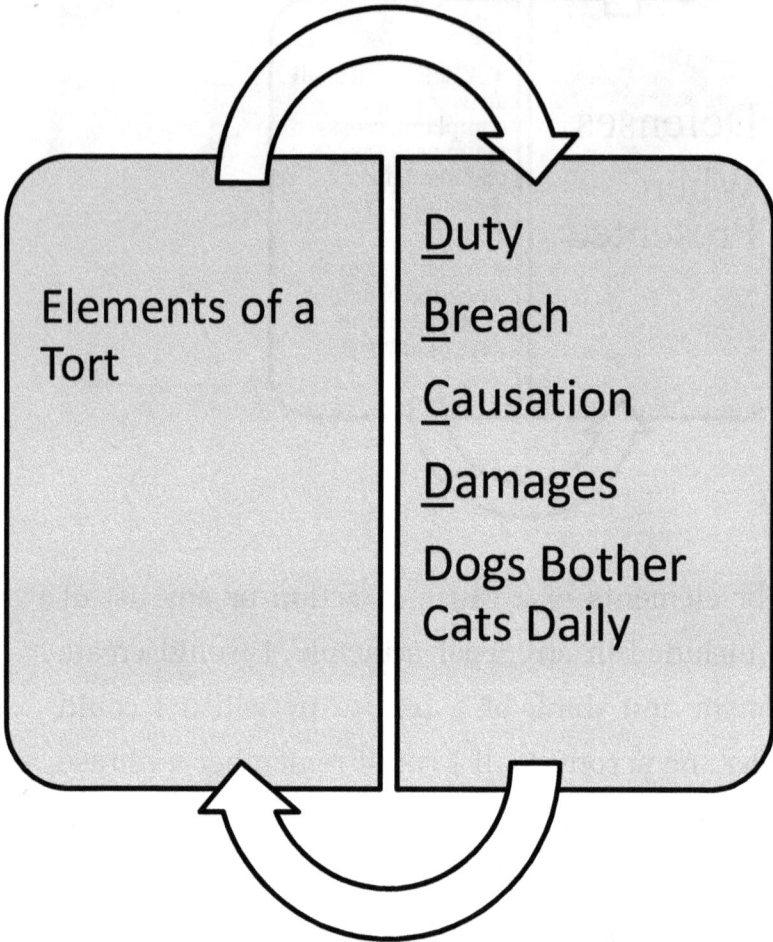

Elements of a Tort

Duty

Breach

Causation

Damages

Dogs Bother Cats Daily

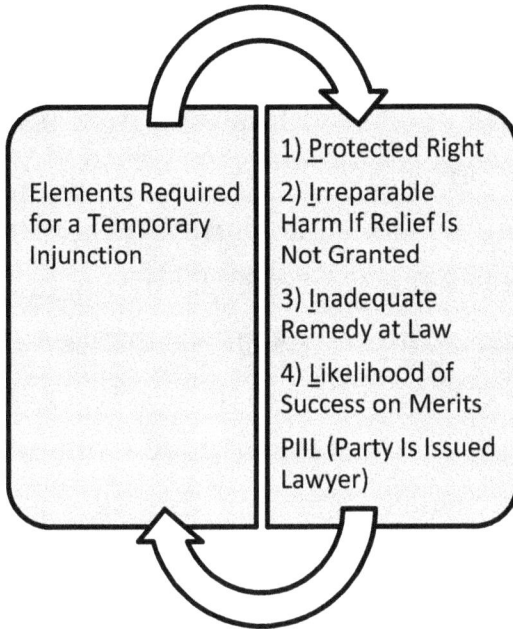

Elements Required for a Temporary Injunction	1) Protected Right
	2) Irreparable Harm If Relief Is Not Granted
	3) Inadequate Remedy at Law
	4) Likelihood of Success on Merits
	PIIL (Party Is Issued Lawyer)

Intentional Infliction of Emotional Distress

◈ This tort is recognized in Florida.

◈ Physical impact or physical manifestation of psychological trauma is not required to state a claim

- Contrast: Florida is generally in accord with the majority view on this point when it comes to negligent infliction of emotional distress

◈ Claim may not be based on privileged defamation

My study routine was soon carved out thus: I would wake up in the morning and go to my BarBri course which began at 9. The class went from 9 to 12, with a ten-minute break every hour. A departure I took from the rest of the students during these breaks, most of whom hovered around the classroom, halls or made a quick trip to the restroom, was by going into the student lounge where VH1 was invariably on. I was almost always the only student in there. One of the maintenance crew usually hung out there during this time, and we would watch such videos as Usher's "Burn," Joss Stone's "Super Duper Love," or Ashlee Simpson's "Pieces of Me."

These brief respites into popular culture gave my brain a welcome break from the constant blitz of information, and by then music was a rare luxury anyway. Even in the car I would constantly have an audio class on of some sort. I tried to leave no moment wasted, but the proximity of the student lounge and the contained entertainment forum it offered was like a fleeting oasis of summer fun which gave me strength to press on.

After BarBri was over, I would jump in my car and drive from Nova back to Coral Springs, listening to a multi-state Torts or Contracts lecture along the way. Upon my return to our subletted room, I would grab a quick lunch, then settle down to my study table with my books and earplugs, with my husband usually lounging in the room behind me watching sports. He has always taken a wonderful *laissez-faire* attitude towards my scholastic and professional duties.

I would then launch into the multi-state practice questions and often test myself under timed conditions. I would take practice tests for the rest of the afternoon, usually until dinnertime. After dinner time I would review my state flashcards for a few more hours and sometimes ask my husband to quiz me on the cards. My study cut-off point was 10 p.m., at which point I would either go to bed right away, listen to the radio for a little while or watch a quick show. There was no nightlife, dancing or partying.

I did not always have perfect days. For example, on the Fourth of July I knocked off my studies a bit early, studying four hours instead of my usual ten. My husband, our roommates and I spent some time on a rooftop parking lot, listening to music and watching the fireworks. On the next day of BarBri, I stopped into a Dunkin' Donuts on the way to class and ran into a fellow classmate. "How was your Fourth of July?" I asked her. "I was studying - you weren't?" she replied haughtily.

I got organized by making lists of all the subjects I had to study (some of which might be on the test, some maybe not) and making a chart of what I would study when:

Log of Subjects To Be Studied

Florida Subjects														
CivPro		□				□				□				□
CrimPro	□		□		□			□				□		
Corps			□		✎	□							□	□
Conlaw					□				□	□				
Equity			□	□			✎	□			□	□		
Famlaw			□	□			□	□					□	□
P'ship				✎	□				□			□		
PR						✎	□		□	□				
Trusts		□						□			✎	□		

Wills	☐	☐				☐	☐			✎	☐			
CrimLaw									☐					
Evidence			☐	☐	☐								☐	☐
Property			☐	☐			☐							
Torts				☐							☐	☐		
<u>**MS Subjects**</u>														
Property			🕐						🕐	🕐				
Evidence											🕐		🕐	
Contacts												🕐		
ConLaw						🕐	🕐							

CrimLaw				⊕									
Torts								⊕	⊕				⊕

This chart represents a study schedule for a two-week period; at which point I had already been studying full throttle for about a month and a half. There is a column for each day, and the marks below indicate what subject will be studied on that day and in what method. The □ symbol meant that I would study that subject by reviewing and testing myself on flashcards. The ✍ meant that I would be preparing a timed essay; for this particular test we would only be required to write essays on state subjects. And finally, the ⊕ indicated that I would be taking a timed test, usually for the PMBR multiple choice questions.

I was studying for the bar shut away in my room for most of the day, occasionally coming out to chat with my roommates in the shared living room and kitchen, until 10 p.m. came and I could hang out for a bit, maybe watch a half hour show. Sometimes loud visitors came to the apartment, bellowing away on their cell phones. I worked with ear plugs almost the entire time and luckily they were pretty good, so even the shouting was faint enough so that I could continue working. I tried not to get up from the table more than once an hour – not to go to the restroom, get a snack, answer the phone, anything.

In the last week or so before the bar exam, I realized I wasn't going to be able to pack much more into my head; in retrospect, this was probably an indication that I had studied enough, although I had no idea at the time. I still did the timed PMBR tests every day, but I stopped trying to study new material or concepts I did not understand very well, such as the infamous property law against perpetuities. I just went over the tried-and-true material; I may have also stopped studying a few subjects which I did not think would be on the test. This phase of the studying was a bit easier now because after I had done the timed tests, I could just sit on the couch with my roommates around; maybe even listen to music while I went through my flashcards.

A classmate and I arranged to drive up to Tampa for the bar exam together and share a hotel room to defray the costs. Upon arrival at the hotel, it looked like a law school reunion, though our class had only been apart for about a month or so. But the gathering was without the jubilance and partying of a reunion. Everyone was tense. Many of us acknowledged each other just like we were co-workers in an office building, taking each other's presence for granted.

The hotel room was reasonably pleasant, with a balcony overlooking a river. I didn't bother to study. I had reached that point when I knew my brain could not hold any more data. The evening started off well enough. My roommate and I went to dinner, and then got back to the room around 7 p.m. I went out onto the balcony, called my husband, then attempted to turn in around 9 p.m., as the exam would start at 9 a.m. and I wanted to get up around 7.

No such luck. Anxiety consumed me. Not helping matters was the fact that my roommate didn't seemed concerned with getting any sleep, as she sat and watched hour after hour of TV. When I asked her, "Aren't you tired?" her breezy response was "I'm a night owl."

I tried standing out on the balcony for a while, forcing myself to stay up so that maybe I would get tired. I called my husband numerous times lamenting my plight and that we had not simply come up together to share a room, so that I would not have to suffer the constant noise. I didn't even bother asking my roommate to turn off the TV - getting into an argument with her and suffering additional stress was the last thing I needed. So I continued my torturous pacing back and forth, lying down sometimes, only to get up again at fifteen minute intervals.

Sometime around 5 a.m. I was so forlorn and fatigued that sleep was able to finally set in, only to be cut short about an hour and a half later. I called my husband and told him that I'd gotten next to no sleep and that I was on my way to the exam site in the Tampa Convention Center.

I joined the stream of students flowing through the downtown sidewalks to the convention center. We walked through the doors to find a sea of chairs, tables and aisles. Somewhere in the distance there appeared to be a podium from which a woman was making announcements and would later give time warnings while we were taking the tests.

We were assigned seats and took our places. We were required to fill out numerous certifications. At one point the certifications were given back to us because we all had to make some correction to them. A former classmate sitting in front of me, the same one who had chastised me about my Fourth of July study routine in the Dunkin' Donuts, suddenly turned around and demanded to me, "Why do I have your signed sh*t?" She was holding my certification I was supposed to correct. In my grogginess I had no idea how or why she had it. I was just swimming along in a daze, knowing the only thing I really had to wake up for in my mind were the questions. I was so insulated by this daze that her barbed comments, which might have otherwise worked in upsetting me and throwing my concentration off, just drifted away down the slow river of my consciousness. This serves as a note to the wise nonetheless; even in the bar exam itself you may face the same vicious, catty competition that prevailed in law school, with the attendant intimidation and harassment. In retrospect, when I saw this student was seated nearby, I might have asked one of the exam monitors to change my seat – but then again, I might not have. I presumed that everyone would just focus on the exam and nothing else, and act like professionals. After it happened, it just seemed like too much trouble to try to move than not try to rock the boat and distract myself.

After seven years, I can no longer remember the substance of anything on the exam; just that the questions and my responses seemed to flow by in a constant determined stream. I also differed from virtually all of my colleagues in my exam attire – while most wore sweats, jeans, T-shirts and some borderline pajama outfits, I wore a business blouse, skirt and moderate heels. I felt that if I dressed in a business-like fashion, my mind would follow suit and get the job done.

After the exam was over, I did not bother standing around poring over the exam with others, quizzing each other on how we might have answered specific questions out of the hundreds. My roommate and I just headed onto the long road back to Coral Springs. After that my husband and I went on a little vacation around Florida, going to Key West, Naples, Orlando and Tampa, to show him the battleground where I did not even know yet who had won the war.

Chapter 12: Miami Associate

A little over a month later, that exulted moment came when I went down to a local library to use a public computer, my terrified eyes followed the line from my exam number, only to find "Pass, Pass" on the two portions of the exam.   I fell to my knees and hugged my husband wildly.   He thought I'd failed at first!

[48]Next, my fledgling career as an attorney would take me to Miami, a city with unique tangible electricity. The job actually began as a temporary assignment, where I was called upon to

---

[48] Thank you to the late great Chad A. Wade for this concept – he always told us to dress this way whenever we went to networking events.

make a report of any files in danger of court dismissal for lack of activity. This was largely an organizational, clerical task, based on a civil procedural rule that a court can dismiss a case in its own discretion if there has been no record activity in a case for a year.[49] This is currently a tool used often by the courts in the foreclosure crisis, to purge stagnant cases from their rosters when a bank fails to prosecute a foreclosure for any number of reasons (transient or ineffective counsel, loan transfers, loss mitigation, etc.).

Make sure you always read and abide by your particular judges rules and procedures. along with the court rules and the law of your jurisdiction

---

[49] Fla. R. Civ. P. 1.420(e).

I first began by getting organized. This was a fairly discrete task, based on a finite number of files, with my assignment expected to end within a week. I made a chart listing all of the firm files, making a note of the last activity within each case, whether such activity was sufficient to prevent dismissal under the civil rule, whether the age of such activity was a year or more, and whether the court had issued an order of dismissal or a notice of intent to issue such an order.

There were no paperless files, but one electronic tool I used to help monitor the cases for the first time was the online docket. Most likely, the date of the last file activity according to this docket would be the reference point the court would use to determine compliance with the procedural rule. The Miami-Dade Clerk of the Court website, by that time, permitted the public to view dockets for cases, in a convenient extension of databases some courts maintained which permitted one to obtain the same information while at the courthouse. Other courts were following this trend to make dockets and case information available to the public online. This trend has expanded such that today virtually all Florida courts maintain an online public docket, with some even allowing free public viewing and download of actual court-filed documents such as in Manatee County.

I expressed hopes to my supervisor that I could continue temping for the firm and help out with another assignment. There was certainly no shortage of work, so they enlisted me to help a paralegal organize and index a voluminous case over ten years old. This task largely drew upon skills and efficiency learned on my coding assignments; to recognize and record specific fields of data. A case index should be maintained on the top of every hard paper file, if one is maintained, and on your hard drive. The most helpful format is usually reverse-chronological order, because then anyone picking up the file can see what was done or what happened most recently:

Tab No.	Document Date	Title of Document	Author	Recipient	Event or Deadline Dates

Every document in a file should be tabbed and indexed in this way. You will then have a timeline of documents which shows what, where, when and why. By adding event or deadline dates derived from the body of the documents, your case index serves as another to-do list. While it should not be relied upon as your only to-do list, as you still need your calendar and appointment book to make sure you stay on top of your events and deadlines, having key dates in your index is useful because you can use the tabs as a quick reference to the documents for assistance in completing the tasks.

My supervisors and attorneys continued to be pleased with my work, so they began introducing new challenges to see how I would rise to the occasion. They began asking me to research legal issues and questions as they came up in the course of the day. I knew how to use both Westlaw and Lexis and I would set out to find cases on all fours with the situation, if any. At that time I was not aware of the option to do key word or issue searches which would cover an entire category of a topic. I would always begin my searches with single words or phrases using connectors and expanders.   I would usually find applicable cases quickly and, once having found these cases, be led to other relevant cases citing the first opinion.

It had not yet occurred to me that I could use keyword searches. In Westlaw and Lexis, the keyword page contains an extensive list of topics and subtopics which lead to cases containing that keynote subject. I am not sure why this research technique had been lost on me throughout law school - but in the real world, you will find you have often overlooked simple work tools which should have been obvious, but some things you can only realize through practical work experience.

So, once I began doing keyword searches, this made my job infinitely easier. If I did not find the cases I needed simply by looking at the results for a topic or subtopic, I would enter in additional search criteria within that topic, such as terms, expanders, dates, phrases, etc.

Other essential research standbys were the state law journal (in my case, Florida Jurisprudence) and American Jurisprudence. These were great resources if I was asked to research a question or topic with which I had no familiarity, and, as a first-year associate, this happened quite often. I would browse through the topic and its various chapters within the jurisprudence, review the cases cited in the footnotes, then examine the procedural history of those cases to gain additional relevant authorities. I learned quickly that while citing the actual jurisprudence journal itself was usually the most direct way of supporting my legal propositions, it was still bad form in practice and a rookie mistake. The senior partner once said to me, "I don't rely on Florida Jurisprudence, and you should not either." In law school, you learn that "[t]he law in the USA is only expressed in constitutions, statutes, and opinions of appellate courts, which are known as primary sources. Secondary sources collect and explain rules of law from the primary sources."[50] Therefore, we should only cite to primary authorities to support our arguments, but the secondary authorities help us to understand the primary ones and to discern directions we should take in research.

I soon had a wide array of assignments, ranging from researching single questions, following up on

---

[50] Ronald B. Standler, Legal Research and Citation Style in USA, (2004), available at http://www.rbs0.com/lawcite.htm.

phone exchanges with people from whom I needed information and assistance, to managing entire cases and pushing them forward, under the review of the partners. The issues included partnerships, property rights, torts, county tax disputes, family law and other matters.

I also began to cover basic hearings, such as motions for continuance, opposition to a motion to strike affirmative defenses and opposition to a pro se motion to dismiss. All of these went smoothly and I was given even more responsibilities and complex cases on my workload.

Be A Detective At Law

A case soon came in which I learned how absolutely important it is that you know everything about your case, which often includes information you do not have in your file yet. Back then the Internet and the access of to all possible worlds of data which might affect your case were not as advanced as they are now, and we may not have been able to perform good detective work on our case by simply sitting at our computer. However, sometimes today this is not even possible either.

This is when you have to take to the streets and visit all the sites which may bear the information you're looking for. When I was a kid, that might have meant going to the library to look up old newspaper articles on microfiche. In our case, we should have gone to the office of the county recorder of public records and examined them for anything that might have related to our issue. Today, many jurisdictions allow online searches of their public records, but when this is not possible you will have to go to the office and go through the physical files.

Some people also hire a private investigator to do extra digging into the facts and unknowns about their case. This is not a bad idea if your client has the means. One of my favorite shows is Matlock, a show that perfectly combines my love of detective work, the law and pure trial lawyer genius. In fact, Matlock and all of his staff always share in the investigating in every show, to perhaps a fictional, sensationalist extent. The lawyers and their investigator all go out in the field to interview witnesses and sometimes engage in high speed pursuits of their subjects as if they were members of law enforcement. While the extent of their pursuits is a bit incredulous and often might not be permitted by local statutes and bar association rules in real life, one message conveyed by their pursuits is that truth in the courtroom can often be obtained only through careful detective work, skill in interviewing witnesses and attention to the smallest details.

Some firms I have worked for do actually hire private investigators, such as criminal defense and family law offices. They can be an incredible asset because as every attorney knows, sometimes our clients do not tell us everything. Of course, attorneys should not foist all of the investigative work upon their staff, but should, like Matlock, actually go into the field to, for example, look at the scene of the accident or crime or review the public records as some information can only be fully interpreted by attorneys or highly trained staff. This way, attorneys can truly dig deep, be thorough, and ascertain as many facts about their case as possible.

There may be information out there that not only helps our case, but also hurts it and we should find the negative information before our opposition does and uses it to blow us out of the water, as was the case in one actual hearing I attended with this Miami office. Opposing counsel had gone through the public records and at the hearing, completely caught us off guard, as he intended, by producing a public document about which neither we nor our client were aware, and which was completely fatal to our argument.

Chapter 13: A Hybrid Contractor/Associate

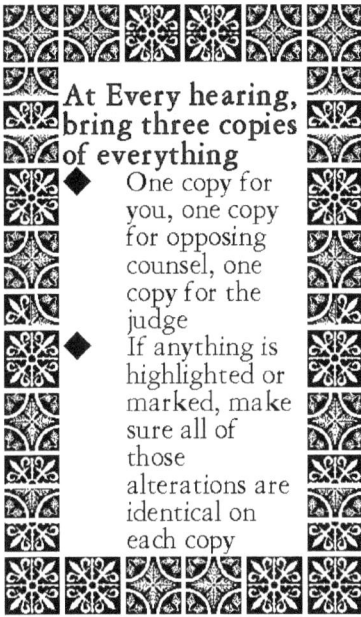

At Every hearing, bring three copies of everything

♦ One copy for you, one copy for opposing counsel, one copy for the judge

♦ If anything is highlighted or marked, make sure all of those alterations are identical on each copy

In my second year of law practice, I once again transitioned to a new career opportunity. It was an interesting arrangement; I was signing on to be an independent contract attorney for a solo practitioner, Mr. Howe.[51] He was engaging me to work on his own office matters, but also permitted me to run my own practice from his office space. This seemed like a fantastic set-up, as I then had a few clients of my own and wanted to continue my own business, but needed some supplemental income.

Surrounding Yourself With the Right Bosses

I noticed right away that Mr. Howe was engaged solely with business development, as many attorneys are who are established business owners or firm partners. This was a bit of a change for me, as I had

---

[51] Name has been changed.

previously been used to my supervising attorneys working hand-in-hand with me on projects, while they were not necessarily jointly responsible for completing the assignment.   For example, other supervisors worked with me hands-on in drafting documents, training me on legal theories and techniques, and briefing me on clients and files.

Hitting the ground running was nothing new for me so I jumped right into reviewing files and determining what needed to be done. Most of them were extremely disorganized and urgently needed action.   The paralegals began coming to me with frantic questions and issues, such that a client was on the phone and demanded to know what we were doing on his case. For a while, such inquiries involved client names I was hearing for the first time and for whose cases I was concurrently learning that I was responsible.

The paralegals were also known as case managers there, meaning they were the contact points for clients and were apparently tasked with deciding what to do next with a file by management.   I immediately informed the paralegals that they could come to me with any questions and implored them not to make any legal determinations on a file without checking with me or another attorney. I soon learned the full extent of how the paralegals had been running cases, often without any attorney oversight. Because there were often matters or questions in cases which the paralegals honestly knew they could not answer, they would constantly have to tell clients that they were waiting for attorney guidance. By the time I arrived at this firm, many such matters had been sitting for weeks or months without any progress for these reasons.

I soon learned that this law firm had a "business development" team which consisted primarily of non-lawyers. The firm's main marketing campaign was via their website, and calls would steadily flow in from all across Florida, sometimes from other states as well. The firm staff would handle these calls with the intention of making a sale by the conclusion of the conversation, by way of taking an initial retainer payment of at least $5,000.00 by credit card. Once they had made the sale and collected the retainer, Mr. Howe would effectively wash his hands of the case and relegate it to the paralegals and the applicable associate, namely me, to handle.

The story gets worse in regard to Mr. Howe, but it can serve as a cautionary tale to attorneys and legal professionals everywhere that you must be careful about whom you get involved with, in business, as a partner, an associate, legal assistant, paralegal or an employee in any capacity. Obviously times are tough, and many people would be happy to have *any* job, regardless of how the employers run their offices or how many ethical violations they have committed. But the integrity of professionals with whom you work can have a grave impact on your career, both present and future.

You can start by looking an attorney up in the local bar association listings or website, and determining whether he has been subject to any bar discipline or negative action, and why. Find out as much about the circumstances as you can and don't rush to judgment. Sometimes it may be arguable whether the bar action was justified. Sometimes the attorney may have made a mistake but has made amends in compelling, demonstrable ways.

You can also look an attorney up on Avvo.com; many attorneys now have an Avvo rating on a scale of one to ten, based on a proprietary algorithm, and clients may also post reviews of experiences with their attorneys. Also ask around amongst your friends and professional colleagues to hear their opinions about a lawyer, which may be very different from what you read online.

Most job postings will not tell you anything about the integrity and ethical standards of the employers, because it is often assumed that job candidates must answer to the employers instead of the other way around, that it is presumptuous for candidates to question employers about their professionalism and honesty. However, candidates are perfectly justified in doing so, as the integrity of their employers can often help make or break their careers. It may not always be a good idea to directly question an employer about

> If your GPA is over 3.0, put that on your resume, otherwise people will assume it's lower

such matters during an interview. However, when you are doing your due diligence about a company to learn information to skillfully field one of the interview toughies, "What do you know about this company?," you are also learning what others have to say about this company and whether taking a job there will actually serve your best interests as well as those of your prospective employer.

The firm had files from all reaches of Florida. While with the firm, I travelled to courthouses in Viera, New Port Richey, Orlando, Miami, Fort Lauderdale, West Palm Beach and others. For most of my assignments, it was my first time handling the issues at hand, which included bitter family, probate and guardianship disputes, mediations, child support arrearage hearings, temporary restraining order mini-trials. These were truly sink-or-swim situations. I had only been practicing law for about two years at this point, and I was also in the third trimester of pregnancy with my son. Yet I found myself thrown into the thick of litigation, against often quite contentious adversaries.

Guardianship

One such matter involved a guardianship case in which we represented the adoptive daughter of an elderly woman who had been adjudicated incompetent and was caught in the middle of a vicious tug-of-war between her son, daughter and other members of the family. As a guardianship matter, the case was assigned to the probate division of the court and opposing counsel had a long standing history with the case and relationships with the judge. There were at least three other attorneys – counsel for the son, counsel for the ward, and counsel for the court-appointed guardian – all of whom vehemently opposed almost every wish of my client.

I made several trips to the distant courthouse on my own to meet with the client and handle hearings in the case. It was an extremely emotional matter for everyone involved and I faced a wall of opposition from the other attorneys and usually the court as well. As I had already seen from my brief experience in another guardianship matter, cronyism can often play a large part in how cases are decided in probate court. For example, in the other matter, where opposing counsel had already been in the case for about two years, I would sometimes take a motion before the court and be told by the judge that he would not grant my client or I any relief unless opposing counsel had agreed to it first. This was ludicrous to me - after all, parties usually do not come before a court in the first place if they can agree on a matter. But these were the constraints in which I had to operate in that case, and the circumstances were not unlike those in my new case representing the daughter.

On one trip to the court, I was to handle an evidentiary hearing to seek expanded visitation of the ward by her daughter, which of course was also opposed by the three other parties. There I was, eight months pregnant, standing in the middle of what felt like a gladiator's pit, conducting cross-examinations of witnesses for the first time. For a while it felt like disaster in the making, but the result was better than what   I   could   have   hoped   for   -   the

> If someone is covering one of your hearings for you, be courteous and prep the file for them
>
> Have a little memo in the file summarizing what the issues are, explaining the caselaw, any helpful tips, the time, date, location of the hearing

judge reserved ruling until another hearing date by which time I would already be on maternity leave and another attorney would be forced to appear on our client's behalf.

Divorce and Child Custody

In another case, I was introduced to some of the ugliness that can often emerge in family law cases, particularly disputes involving children. Of all the litigation I have ever come across, some of the most bitter and hateful disputes between litigants have been those between spouses and even other family members. It can be shocking to realize that sometimes the closest people to us in our life, the ones with whom we share childhood memories, build homes together, create and raise children, share the holidays and celebrate life, can become our worst enemies to a nightmarish extent.

The case involved a divorcing couple who shared only one biological child among several children in the family. The shared child was the only one about whose custody the spouses fought bitterly. The case involved spiteful calls to the Department of Children and Families (DCF), flight with the subject child to a homeless shelter amongst allegations of abuse, and obstructions of visitation rights.

For one hearing, it appeared to me that I would need to subpoena several witnesses. I had never used the subpoena power before and I would soon learn that it was not as simple a matter as having the subpoena served and the witness showing up. Once I received returns of service for all subpoenas, the calls of protestation began. The witnesses complained that they were not available, that they had family conflicts, that it was too far for them, etc. The DCF witnesses got their in-house counsel involved in challenging the subpoenas. I insisted to everyone that we needed their presence to help establish the factual violations that had occurred, and the whole time I was thinking that I should not have to explain myself this much to witnesses legally required to attend this hearing, and who had not even filed any written opposition. It was one of my many experiences to underscore that no matter how invincible and authoritative attorneys may think they are, others often do not see them that way.

One approach that I have seen more seasoned attorneys take with subpoenaing witnesses is that they will call the witness before issuing a subpoena and attempt to secure their voluntary cooperation. However, even if a witness gives you the most compelling verbal assurance that he will appear at a hearing without a subpoena, you are risking the very good possibility that he will not show up, playing Russian Roulette with your client's case and potentially committing malpractice.   I remain firmly convinced that all subpoenas for that hearing were necessary, but if the same situation happened now I would not have wasted any time arguing with witnesses about whether they should attend.   Unless a witness files a motion to quash the subpoena or any other document that may be required to oppose the subpoena and the court grants the witness relief, having such conversations with witnesses is counter-productive.   Hardly anyone likes being compelled to appear in court and testify anyway.

✤ **Before A Deposition or Other Potentially Hazardous Event, Make Sure Your Client Fully Understands What To Expect**

✤ Fully prep them on the sorts of questions they could be asked and have a dry run-through, do proactive damage control

✤ After it's over, have a pow-wow to determine where you go from here, make sure you are on the same page; if there are any hard feelings, potential fall-out or complaints, deal with them right away so that your business relationship is not jeopardized

Depositions

Another issue I encountered was having a client walk out of her own deposition when certain individuals appeared there, who had not been previously disclosed as attending, with whom my client had extremely bitter relations. The other individuals were named parties to the action so at least on the spot, I was willing to concede that they had a right to be there. However, if my client and I had known beforehand that these parties planned to attend, I would have filed a motion for protective order so as to save my client from an explosively volatile deposition environment and added burden and harassment. As it was, I had to chase my client out onto the street, beg and plead with her to go back in because the other side would have loved to seek sanctions against her for non-appearance, and eventually calm her down enough for her to reenter.

Stopping a Foreclosure Sale via Federal Court

I also experienced my first foreclosure defense matter, in the form of an emergency. One morning, I had just come into the office and was told that we had a new client, his home was scheduled to be sold at the state courthouse that morning at 11 a.m., that he wanted to save the home and our plan was to file a complaint in federal court alleging various Truth in Lending Act (TIL) violations, also demanding injunctive relief in order to stop that morning's sale. At that point in my career, I had only prepared one motion for injunction, or temporary restraining order, but the time frame had been nowhere near as immediate, and I had had the chance to review and refine numerous drafts of the motion with my supervisor. I knew nothing about motions to cancel sale or even the possibility of such relief, as I would later learn at the foreclosure firms. I also had no clue as to how to prepare a complaint for TIL violations and had only about two hours to prepare all the paperwork, figure how to get it directly to the judge and possibly have the judge rule on our motion before the sale took place.

I immediately plunged into the research for the complaint and motion, and just took the first few federal lending statutes I could find, figuring that I could simply amend the complaint at a later date. I took the first form for a complaint I could find and began copying and pasting the relevant information into the form. As fast as I could, I also dug up a bare-bones form for an injunction motion and began filling in the minimum allegations I needed to assert a claim for injunctive relief, tracking the required elements for a federal injunction:

> Whether a preliminary injunction should issue involves consideration of (1) the threat of irreparable harm to the movant; (2) the state of the balance between this harm and the injury that granting the injunction will inflict on other parties litigant; (3) the probability that movant

> will succeed on the merits; and (4) the
> public interest.[52]

Once I had cobbled together the most basic complaint and motion which could still express what we needed and when, I had a runner dispatched to the federal court to file the complaint and motion so that we could be issued a case number and be assigned to a judge. After the runner called me and gave me the judge's name, I immediately looked up his number and was connected with his judicial assistant. I asked if I could have the complaint and motion faxed in to the judge so that he could rule on it before the sale took place. The judicial assistant said that they did not typically allow materials to be faxed to the judge's office, but that he would speak with the judge about it and call me back.

Thankfully, a short time later, he called me back, said the judge would review our complaint and motion, and gave me the fax number, warning me the number was for this one-time use. And a few minutes before the sale was scheduled to occur, we received an order

---

[52] <u>Dataphase Systems, Inc. v. CL Systems, Inc.</u>, 640 F. 2d 109, 113 (8th Cir. 1981). It may not be a bad idea to memorize these elements, as I was once quizzed on the requirements for an injunction in an interview and could remember all but one.

by fax from the judge's office. The order took note of the bare-bones nature of our filings but stated that we had made sufficient allegations to warrant cancellation of the sale so that our client did not suffer the injury of losing his home before his complaint could even be answered by the defendant.

Emergency Mediation

On another occasion, I was sent to court on the day that final judgment was to be entered in a divorce case. Mr. Howe did not think that the judgment would be favorable to our client at all and urged me to move for a continuance or say we wanted to go to mediation, anything to prevent the judgment from being entered. I went down to the courthouse to find our client with her very irate daughter, who berated me about her having to leave two sick children in Texas behind to attend the proceedings.

We finally entered the courtroom after waiting behind dozens of other litigants. Opposing counsel began his argument to enter judgment, but I cut him off and stated we wanted to go back to mediation. I had no specific legal or factual argument on my side and truly did not know what I was doing, other than to say that our client was willing to work something out, which was true. The judge was irritated that we were bringing up this argument now out of the blue. Opposing counsel stated that we had tried to work things out before but such negotiations had been unsuccessful. Nonetheless, he begrudgingly said he was willing to try again if our client was serious. I told the judge we would find a mediator who was available that same day and have the case resolved, though I had no idea how this would happen.

Opposing counsel actually volunteered the name of a mediator who happened to be available that afternoon, someone neither my client nor I knew anything about. However, he seemed to be our only chance. My motion calendar morning down at the court house expanded into the afternoon as I rushed over to the mediator's office, not stopping for lunch or as much as a snack. Ultimately, the case did settle, in only two hours, approximately, and I was able to keep my promise to the judge on which I had no idea at the time how I would deliver.

Delinquent Child Support

Another close shave happened when I was told I would have to go to a child support hearing, where it was alleged that our client owed thousands of dollars in back child support. Though I was perhaps blithely unaware at the time, it was possible our client could have gone to jail that day. We sat in a small conference room where an assistant state attorney sat in front of a judge at a table and monotoned through the argument of case after case, as if she were speaking to a coworker. My client and I inwardly gasped as we watched the judge entered order after order imposing substantial child support debts.

My client had brought with him several account statements and receipts accounting for payments he had made, though they did not account for the entire time he was alleged to be delinquent. I called him to testify to fill in the gaps. The judge questioned him about his monthly expenses, in which my client stated he and his new wife were essentially in poverty, never so much as going out to eat. The judge stated that my client would receive credit for the money he was able to account for, and ultimately rescheduled the matter for a later date so that my client could retrieve other evidence of payment. My client and I were ecstatic, as we both had thought that a "sentence" would have been imposed that day for sure.

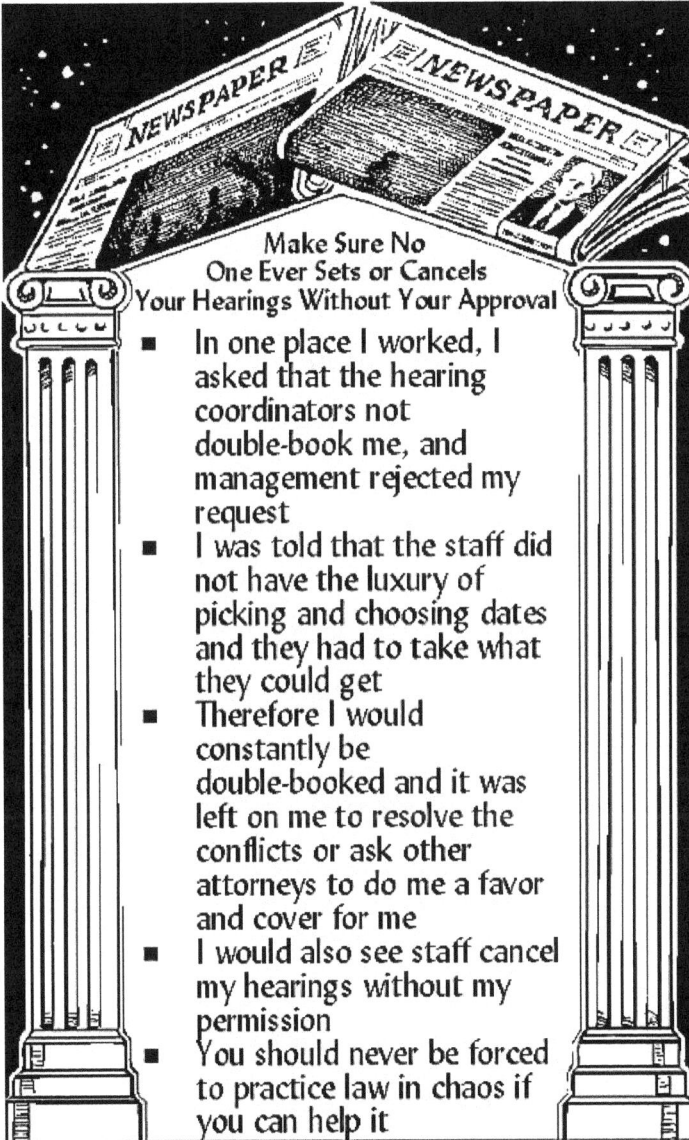

Make Sure No One Ever Sets or Cancels Your Hearings Without Your Approval

- In one place I worked, I asked that the hearing coordinators not double-book me, and management rejected my request
- I was told that the staff did not have the luxury of picking and choosing dates and they had to take what they could get
- Therefore I would constantly be double-booked and it was left on me to resolve the conflicts or ask other attorneys to do me a favor and cover for me
- I would also see staff cancel my hearings without my permission
- You should never be forced to practice law in chaos if you can help it

Chapter 14: Mastering Foreclosure Volume

Learning how to deal with volume as an attorney is a valuable skill. Obviously, the goal is to maintain speed and accuracy. Before you start working, however, it is crucial to get organized. A friend of mine once told me that "The key to happiness is organization." While organization doesn't solve all of life's problems, it certainly can go a long way towards happiness in work and home. As far as work is concerned, organization helps you prioritize, know what you need to tackle each day, what must be done and by when, and what is optional for a given day. When you work under the guidelines of a system, whether devised by you or someone else, you have better chances of completing your tasks, having the peace of mind of knowing you put in a good day's work, and a more satisfying transition into recreation mode.

Often, as a new associate, you will arrive on the job and essentially be thrown to the wolves. Your new boss is most likely overwhelmed with work and hopes you will be able to hit the ground running so as to minimize the company time and money lost while you are trained. This is where it pays to be adept in organization and often, in handling volume. When I arrived to work for a bank foreclosure firm a few years ago, the office was inundated with work, which is still the case in the so-called "default" industry to this day. My supervising attorney did spend a fair amount of time with me explaining some important laws which would govern how to handle certain court papers and inherent deadlines therewith. He also explained how to handle and respond to the first few documents in a voluminous stack of mail. However, the rest of the stack was left up to me.

I started out by determining the structure, if any, that was already in place. One good thing was that, even in the midst of stacks of haphazard papers and the chaotic bustle of the office, I had a defined caseload. My supervisor would either bring me a file or email me with case documents for a matter that was now assigned to me. He also told me that I might receive as many as seventy-five new files in one week. I immediately began to prepare a Microsoft Excel spreadsheet, with columns labeled as such:

Case Name and Matter No.	Date Received	Client	Notes

I was not sure at this point whether I would need more headings than just these four, but for the time being this was my start in getting a handle on things. Ultimately, even when my caseload list rose as high as five hundred, I never added more columns than these. When dealing with an extremely high volume of cases, the caseload template I introduced in Chapter 10 is not practical. In this kind of situation, I could see that it would be best to primarily use my calendaring tool for management of my cases, because deadlines were occurring on a daily basis.

So, I began going through the stacks of documents and looking for any kind of deadlines or events that needed to be calendared. This is normally a secretarial task which many attorneys do not deign to touch but it had to be done. I had been introduced to a woman who would be my assistant but I was told that she would be in training for at least a week or so and I was not told of anyone else who would be doing calendaring.

Calendaring was also a job which I felt I could do fairly quickly and efficiently, and I would only be helping my productivity and quality of work in the end. When I first began my legal career in that Newark assignment, I learned how to zero in on certain pieces of information in documents, such as dates, and handle that information quickly. Now, years later, I knew a great deal more about the documents I was looking at, but this was the time to go back to basics.

I began sifting through all letters, pleadings and court documents to check for hearing dates, mention of laws which invoked particular deadlines, discovery and other documents to which a response was mandated by law within a certain time. At the time, the calendaring tool I used was Outlook. The advantages of that program included the fact that Outlook was also my email program, and I was already using the program constantly throughout the day. For Outlook to be most effective for calendaring purposes, I would need to check my calendar at the beginning of the day and make note of the day's deadlines. Outlook also allows you to print out calendars by day, week, month or year. The problem is that with the exception of the day view, Outlook calendar printouts do not allow you to view all relevant details of your appointments as the printout area will usually cut off information which you had included in the original calendar entry. I found that instead of printing out week or month views, I would have to print out individual day calendars for the time period I needed.

My calendar quickly filled up as I continued to enter events from the piles of documents and files on my desk. Soon though, the mountains of paper became less intimidating because a hierarchy of priorities was emerging. Luckily, it was not my job to file all of the documents; somehow other staff made sure that they made their way into my assigned files and that my files could be sorted alphabetically in my office. This firm had not adopted a paperless system for the majority of its documents, though certain categories of items would usually be imaged in their case management system. I had spoken my piece to management about how paperless would be the best way to go for all qualifying documents, including most litigation documents. I attempted to sell them on a system like my personal favorite, Amicus, where every single document, fax, email and even telephone call log can be linked and filed electronically within a specific case. The hard copy purists won out, however.

KEEP A COPY OF YOUR CALENDAR ON YOU AT ALL TIMES, ESPECIALLY THE WHAT, WHERE AND WHEN OF ANY PLACE YOU NEED TO BE THE NEXT MORNING AND TAKE THE FILE HOME WITH YOU IF NECESSARY

Despite not having the added convenience of being able to look up all case documents on my computer and having mounds of files foisted upon my office for me to try to keep neat, I soon fell into a productive rhythm of workflow. When I arrived in the morning, I would open Outlook immediately and note the day's deadlines, determine whether any were negotiable, and get to work on any documents I needed to prepare and send out that day. The mailroom staff maintained a daily deadline of 3:00 to receive any documents to go out in that day's mail. Therefore, I knew that I would have to work on getting documents ready to go first, and that any other non-emergency matters could wait until my document deadlines were completed.

My training supervisor was also available to meet with me every day at 2:00. At that time we would review any questions I had. The meetings were usually brief; only five to ten minutes, which left me plenty of time to finalize any outstanding documents and deliver them to the copy staff prior to 3:00. Once I had made my hand-off, I would then focus on non-emergency emails, responding to them in the order of priority. Outlook also permits a user to flag emails, including response due dates if applicable, and adding such due dates to the user's Outlook to-do list.

If I had hearings in the morning, I would of course arrive at the office later in the day and have less time to prepare my paperwork. On days that I had court, I would try to schedule fewer paperwork deadlines in my Outlook. If a particular court deadline occurred on a busy hearing day, I would be sure to complete that deadline a business day or two prior. Another part of my job regarding hearings was to find another attorney to cover for me if I had hearings scheduled for the same day in different counties, which happened quite frequently. I was often frustrated that the attorneys were called upon to do this instead of having a staff member act as hearing coordinator and decide which attorneys would be where, when. Scheduling matters is really a clerical function and should be handled by staff so a needless level of stress is not added to attorney tasks. Attorneys should be primarily concerned with analytical functions, not logistical matters like scheduling. I knew how to do clerical tasks myself and often did them happily because of my experience. But a law firm, especially an extremely busy one, is likely to run more smoothly if tasks are delegated to the appropriate staff, and no department is asked to perform tasks which would be better and more efficiently performed by another department with more apt training and resources.

Before long my supervisors came to me saying things like, "Management loves you, the higher-ups love you," and "I wish I had ten more of you." It seemed I was leading the pack in production. Many people were getting bogged down in the volume, and many new associates did not last long on the job because they simply couldn't handle the workload. I explained my personal system to the bosses; that barring any emergencies I always worked on what had to get out the door first, and went from there. My supervisors were impressed with my efficiency and quality of work.

I was also meticulous about keeping my billing current, which always kept management and the owners happy because this meant more money in their pocket too. My workstation was set up with double monitors, so I always reserved one screen for my billing sheet and caseload list, where I could flip back and forth easily between the two. I reserved my other screen for Outlook, Microsoft Word and the internal case management system. I organized my billing according to the following categories:

Date	Case Name and Matter No.	Category of Work Performed	Tasks Completed	Hours (in increments of .1)

My personal billing goal for each day was eight hours minimum. My billing was often enhanced by the fact I was completing so many documents, for which I could be credited far more time than a typical phone call or email. Many people struggled to complete documents and get them out the door, let alone organize their time to allow greater focus, preparation and research for a document as warranted. If issues were sufficiently complex, I would conduct research and due diligence until I had the resources to prepare a document at the appropriate level of quality and detail. Many people would rely only on the preexisting document templates circulating amongst us and not bother to create a new document if one did not already exist. Because of my proficiency in creating tailored documents, I was soon called upon frequently by my colleagues to provide them with templates, to which requests I always obliged.

I stuck to my schedule religiously, because there were always distractions attempting to throw me off track. However, my routine was so ingrained that if I was interrupted, I could look at the time of day, my Outlook, know right where I should be, and go right back there. I was so integrated with my system that I could multitask; work on a document, help direct a filing clerk who was looking for something in my office, answer a frantic question from my assistant, respond to an urgent client email, take a phone call, etc.

We frequently had staff and department meetings, while certainly important and often necessary, also threatened to detract from organization and productivity. Our supervisor would bring an agenda of announcements, advice and admonishments, which always sparked additional discussions and questions. While much of this time was valuable, a good portion of it involved questions and discussions which were more for the benefit of their proponents than the group as a whole, and might better have been left for discussion after the meeting was adjourned. Trading discussion and ideas amongst colleagues is usually interesting and valuable, but this too takes time from your work day and accordingly must be prioritized according to your other tasks.

Sometimes you will have corporate clients who operate according to an escalation matrix

They are always accustomed to escalating things and that will even include legal advice you give them

If you have one of those clients who will go over your head the second you tell them something they don't want to hear, before you even talk to this client, talk to your chain of command

If your chain agrees with your position, ask if you can do a conference call with the client where you and your chain are unified in what you tell the client

Chapter 15: Legal Practice

Professional Relationships

One significant lesson I have learned in the legal business is that if you like your job, give it your all, your best, pour your heart into it. Come in as early and stay as late as necessary for you to really own your work, understand every aspect of what you are asked to do, and create masterpieces in your work. And you cannot do it alone. Eventually, you will experience difficulties with your co-workers, perhaps even your superiors.   Set up a meeting with the person in question so that you can attempt to resolve your differences face-to-face.   If that doesn't work right away, seek the help of others in the office. Do not engage in office gossip; perhaps you can invite the other party out to lunch to lighten the air and have a chance to hear each other out. Alternatively, go to someone in authority

Make sure you and your employer are clear on where you stand on family and time to be with them*

*Not medical advice, just my own experience

to discuss the problem and how to reach an amicable solution with the other party without starting a human resource grievance, if possible.

If the job allows almost no room to be with family and family is very important to you, you should look for another job. You would probably be miserable in the end. Make sure your employer knows from the beginning about special family and medical needs you have, such as regular trips to pick your child up from school, doctor's appointments, trips and other unexpected needs that may arise in your personal and family life.

As far as office gossip, it will most likely be everywhere you work; it just goes with the territory. For the most part, just let the gossip roll off your back, you can tolerate it without perpetuating it. Just let the gossipers vent and keep to your work. Even if someone is trying to badmouth you, do not let it distract you. Most likely, if you have not done anything negative to provoke the gossip, the chatter has spawned because you are doing your job well and others who perform at a substandard level see you as a threat. Supervisors and bosses don't need more drama

- they always need more results. Whatever people say about you, if you keep to your work and do your best, your work results will likely speak more in your defense than your dignifying the gossip with a response. Your bosses cannot argue with money. If you are benefitting the company and helping it realize the ultimate, ubiquitous goal of more profits, that is what your bosses will value, not the drama.

Also, there will be the issue of socializing with others in the office. In all my years of experience, I have found that outings with your coworkers, in moderation, with the proper conduct, can actually enhance your relationships with others at work. If you want to go to Happy Hour with the office, do it maybe once a month, drink in moderation, and prearrange for a designated driver or for family or friends to pick you up afterwards. Don't make Happy Hour a habit, where you come to depend on it or need it.

And always keep things professional between you and your coworkers, both male and female alike. One of my bosses advised that "You can be friendly with your coworkers, but not friends with them." This doesn't always follow because I have seen plenty of coworkers be friends and proper on the job. It's hard to know from the beginning, however, whether someone will be a trusted friend for years or if you should always keep an arms-length relationship with them. Before becoming friends with someone at work, it would probably be best to have known and worked with them for at least a year.

And then there's office romance. Of course there are always people who meet their future spouses at work, and those people who can maintain successful romances (those which don't end badly for either party's career) with their coworkers. But these are usually exceptions to the rule. If office romance is more important to you than your career, one of you should be willing and ready to find work elsewhere or work in a different location. There are some people who feel they can only advance in their career through romantic connections rather than professional merit. Of course there are always exceptions to the rule and people who may advance this way temporarily, but their advancement may be short-lived or a negative reputation may ultimately precede them in the long run.

Many people join the practice of law because they like to argue, debate, have analytical minds, and enjoy word-jousting. Sometimes people can remain good sports and sometimes they can't. Much of the practice of law is like a sport, where minds and tongues, rather than muscles are trained, and where usually, one party wins and the other loses. This is not to say that the cases and matters being argued are just trivial games, as sometimes our property, rights, basic liberties and even life can be at stake. But the same emotions can come into play as when you face an adversary in sport.   Often, attorneys are not themselves fighting for each other's lives or even their own rights, but usually those of their clients. Yet, attorneys invest a great deal in their causes; egos, time, energy, sometimes their own money, hope that their reputations and good will with clients will be enhanced, and more. As a result of all of these investments, the stakes can be high when attorneys face off against each other, and they are not always sportsmanlike in winning and losing.

Cases between attorneys do not have to be personal. It is extremely personal for the clients but not necessarily so for the attorneys, unless the rapport between attorneys may facilitate dispute resolution. But it is not long before many attorneys begin sniping and squabbling amongst themselves with no real gain except to escalate tension and stress in their careers. Many attorneys do not use intellect and reason, but intimidation as their first line of defense. Intimidation is usually an inefficient strategy because it will tip your opposition off that they are under attack and likely cause them to dig their heels in deeper.

Also, attorneys sometimes feel that they have to rebut or oppose every dig their opponent makes. Having also been down this road myself many times, I have learned that engaging in petty arguments with opposing counsel just distracts from the quality of work and services you provide your client. As many

> Even if you're not required to wear a business suit to work every day, make sure you keep a suit in your office at all times for emergencies or if you have to cover for someone unexpectedly

lawyers say, all that we have to sell is our time and when we spend it arguing with our opponent, we are losing opportunities to reflect on the best strategies for our clients' cases and pursuing same.

Marketing

In the digital age, attorney services are increasingly expected to be ordered and obtained just like any other product obtainable online. Non-lawyer Chris Miles, who might serve as a good representative of most people needing legal services, has launched a new company called LawyerUp, which can match clients and attorneys within fifteen minutes.[53] One central premise to this company, as declared by Mr. Miles, is ""If I want a pizza, I can get a pizza in 15 minutes...I can get a plumber in the middle of the night. Why can't I get a lawyer?"

Why not, indeed. And now we are able to discern a great deal more about attorneys before we hire them and even obtain "legal advice" from them

---

[53] John Schwartz, <u>Delivering a Lawyer Within 15 Minutes (Soda Extra)</u>, NEW YORK TIMES, June 16, 2011.

first, thanks to companies such as Avvo.[54] Consumers are able to pose questions to attorneys on Avvo, and the questions are then categorized into the appropriate legal field, such as Family Law, Contracts, Foreclosures, etc. When attorneys post answers to these questions, they are then able to add their own customized disclaimer as a footer to their answer, covering attorneys' concerns that their information could be construed as legal advice, etc. Every time attorneys answer questions or post legal essays or articles on Avvo, they earn points and rise up the hierarchy of Avvo's Contributor Levels. And as Avvo states:

More answers, more points

Your name, photo, and a direct link to your profile appear with every answer you post, and you may answer as often as you want. Every posting earns you Contributor Points that could earn you "Top Contributor" billing for your practice area. Top Contributors are featured on all major pages of our website and, not surprisingly, are most often the top-viewed attorneys on Avvo.[55]

---

[54] http://www.avvo.com/. This site also provides information and ratings for doctors and the ability to hold free question and answer sessions with doctors.
[55] http://www.avvo.com/answer-legal-questions

It seems like these days, it is more of a buyer's market everywhere.   For those with the resources, it's a phenomenal time to buy a house.   Attainable price points of popular products, such as the Subway $5 Footlong, have been celebrated and mimicked.   Sites like Groupon and Living Social have spawned which boast of bargains which allow consumers to momentarily escape the pain of this economy and still indulge in their favorite restaurants, bars, treats and get-aways.   And all products can and will be reviewed now, with practically every online shopping outlet and social network inviting and soliciting users to offer reviews.   Everything is under a microscope now; all we have to do is Google, Bing, Yahoo or otherwise search engine a person, product, service or any other thing and receive a wealth of information about them. Businesses must therefore cater to consumers more than ever, because if they don't customers will find negative opinions and feedback about such a company and can most likely find another establishment who will do what it takes to make customers happy overall.

As the founder of Avvo, Mark Britton points out, one of the skills in which law schools do not sufficiently train their students is inter-personal skills, commerce, and dealing with people.[56]   As mentioned earlier, many schools operate as an employee training ground.   When a professor barks at us and demands that we regurgitate back to him the holdings of a case, it is a precursor to having the senior partner similarly confront us about why that summary judgment motion isn't done yet.   In many ways, law school instills the worker-bee mentality in us. I certainly found this to be true at NSU Law, where the culture of gossip approximated that of the workplace.   Students either assimilated with this culture or were branded as pariahs. Assimilation is a survival tool for employees, not business owners.

I share Mr. Britton's consternation with some law schools' rebuttal that they are not business schools and therefore need not train their students in the skills of commerce.   This logic assumes that law school graduates will never be expected to, for example, have client conferences, reassure a frantic client calling into the office that her ex-husband is violating their

---

[56] http://avvoblog.com/2011/07/11/ummmm-you-mean-i-have-to-talk-to-people/

visitation agreement, learn the correct demeanor with which to approach a judge and perhaps more difficult, an antagonistic opposing counsel. Furthermore, many employment positions, particularly with the new scrutiny and selectivity of today's job market, make good inter-personal skills a job requirement.

Getting a job today is already an onerous task, and not just because there are fewer positions available. Employers have also steepened the qualifications and increased the disqualifiers for job candidates. Employers know that more qualified candidates than ever are out of work, so for example, they can obtain another associate for a paralegal or even secretarial salary. They have also added additional hoops through which candidates must jump: passing a background and credit check, increased demand for references, and sometimes excluding anyone who is not already employed, thereby aggravating the unemployment dilemma instead of being part of the solution. Often, companies will not permit job candidates to apply for a position by simply submitting a cover letter and résumé, they force a candidate to create an account and profile on the company website that the candidate will most likely never use again if she does not get the position. Then, the candidate is forced to fill out field after field, page after page of their life story; they must list and describe all of their past and present employment positions individually, even if this information was already furnished in the résumé. The candidate then must do likewise with all of her educational and qualification history, then overcome the arduous questions demanding the applicant to describe, in essay format, why they are qualified for and are the ideal candidate for the position.

All such information could have been requested of a candidate once the company expressed interest in the candidate's résumé, so that the candidate does not waste valuable job search time telling her life story to a company from whom she many never hear from beyond a form email acknowledging acceptance of the application. But in requiring all candidates to provide such extensive personal information to the company directly, the company has often required the candidates to grant licenses allowing the company to

use candidates' personal information for the company's own financial gain and marketing purposes.

And on top of all this, many employers, such as one bank foreclosure firm where I was a contested litigation associate, include good inter-personal skills as part of their job descriptions and requirements. "Good inter-personal skills" in modern times is frequently a euphemism for customer service. How many lawyers would actually want (as opposed to need) a job where one of our required functions is "customer service"? Granted, attorneys must certainly endeavor to be personable and diplomatic with clients, judges, opposing counsel and the public alike; that's just common sense. But customer service between an attorney, a hotel concierge, a receptionist, a restaurant server, an airline pilot, a doctor and other professionals may be completely different, and should be.

The raw, unfiltered definition of customer service I learned over about ten years in the food service industry is the familiar credo "The customer is always right." What does this mean? If a customer takes a sandwich back to you saying "I said no mayo!" even though you clearly heard him say "put mayo on it" when he ordered, you apologize, make him a new one or give him a refund, no questions asked. If you're a waitress (yeah I said waitress, not server – I can say that since I was one) and someone says "Where's my coffee?" you say "Coming right away!" with a smile. If you're offering free soup samples, as I did one time in a New York City bistro and a businessman mockingly mimicks your announcement of "Free Soup!," you just grin right back at him. To deal with the constant degradation food service employees suffer, "kill 'em with a smile" becomes the counter-credo and survival strategy to keep from losing your mind.

What would attorney practice look like if we employed the food service definition of customer service? Professional judgment would go out the window. So much for compliance with such bar regulations as Florida Rule Regulating the Florida Bar 4-5.4, Professional Independence of a Lawyer:

> (d) Exercise of Independent Professional Judgment. A lawyer shall not permit a person who recommends, employs, or pays the lawyer to render legal services for another to direct or regulate the lawyer's professional judgment in rendering such legal services.

Yet attorneys permit their clients to regulate their judgment all the time in rendering professional services, all in the name of customer service. A perfect example of this is, once again, the bank foreclosure law firms. What do you do when you have a client who violates court orders, the rights of the opposing party and refuses reasonable settlements to the litigation? You can withdraw, right? Wrong - not in the foreclosure mill. You must placatingly attempt to wheedle your client into cooperating. If the client does not, too bad - you are stuck with the case anyway, as it is often against the customer service policy of foreclosure mills to withdraw from cases.

Competition for bank foreclosure business is often fierce, rabid and desperate. If you irritate the client on one case by withdrawing or put your foot down and say there can be no more court violations, that client can take their business and thousands of files elsewhere to one of the many eager vendors waiting in the throng, who maintains "The customer is always right" with a smile, even as to legal matters.

The bank foreclosure industry is an extreme example, but it serves as a model for the way all attorneys must conduct their customer service to a certain extent. Just like any other business, product, service or vendor these days, lawyers are subject to the 👍 +1 📱 etc. buttons, as well as the various incarnations of ✦✦✦✦✦ and 👎. If an attorney does not perform to the satisfaction of their clients, commits errors, malpractice or simply just rubs a client the wrong way, chances are the world may hear about it online. In this day and age, attorneys may be well-advised to spell out, and make sure their prospective clients are clear on the attorney's customer service policy prior to proceeding into a business relationship. Certain things that attorneys once assumed would go without saying are no longer necessarily true, such as presuming that clients trust their attorneys to be the expert and to handle legal case strategies in the way the attorneys see fit.

The role attorneys and legal assistants once had in customer service might be analogized to that of airline pilots. Certainly, we have always expected the pilot to have a friendly voice, cordially welcome us aboard, perhaps do a little bit of tour-guiding and point out interesting sights or landmarks below. But we trust the pilot to maneuver the plane and take us safely to our destination. We may get frustrated, even scared or angry at the pilot when, for example, the plane is hitting a lot of air pockets, it feels like we're falling out of the sky and we hear no reassurance from the cockpit. But when we safely land on the tarmac, we understand that the pilot did his job. We don't necessarily need to know how he did it; the fact that he accomplished his goal is all that matters.

Sometimes an attorney/client relationship is more analogous to a pilot/passenger one because the case may involve matters of life and death, as did the highly publicized Casey Anthony trial. Whatever your opinion on the verdict (that's a whole other story) may be, the State of Florida was seeking the death penalty, and perhaps if Ms. Anthony followed her attorney's directions, as airline passengers must follow those

> **If possible, always have a car that is client-ready - You never know when you might be asked to go pick up a client from the airport on a moment's notice**

from their pilot, that compliance may well have saved her life. Sometimes an attorney/client relationship comes nowhere near lives being at stake; it may just relate to personal or property rights, and there is no bright-line limit on the triviality of claims that can be filed in court, as long as there is some good faith legal basis.

But perhaps there was once more implicit trust reposed in attorneys by their clients before the digital age. Logically, if a client decides to hire an attorney, it would follow that the client places enough confidence and respect in that lawyer to competently handle the case as the attorney sees fit, and understand that no legal result is guaranteed.

Now, clients can easily second-guess their attorneys online when things are not going their way, no matter how temporary the setback and regardless of what the attorney's ultimate strategy is. However, lawyers should endeavor to have their clients understand that our customer service cannot be the same as workers in other industries. Perhaps clients should be warned that at times they may, and probably will, feel frustrated and angry at their lawyers.

Legal proceedings, especially litigation, can be like a roller-coaster without the fun. Again, using the Casey Anthony trial as an example, without getting into the divisive subject of whether the result was right or wrong, that entire three-year process was certainly a roller coaster for the defendant, and there may have been times she believed that she would be put to death as the State of Florida was seeking to do. Yet, she was acquitted of all but several misdemeanor charges, credited for time served and released about two weeks after the verdict. Doubtless at times, she must have felt frustrated at the very least with her attorneys. The defense attorneys themselves obviously thought there was a possibility Ms. Anthony could have been

ORGANIZE A
FUN TEAM
EVENT FOR
THE OFFICE
EVERY NOW
AND THEN; IT
COULD BE A
SOFTBALL,
ULTIMATE
FRISBEE,
CHARITY 5-K,
BOWLING
NIGHT, PICNIC,
ETC.

SOMETHING
WHERE
PEOPLE DON'T
HAVE TO
DRINK TO
HAVE A GOOD
TIME

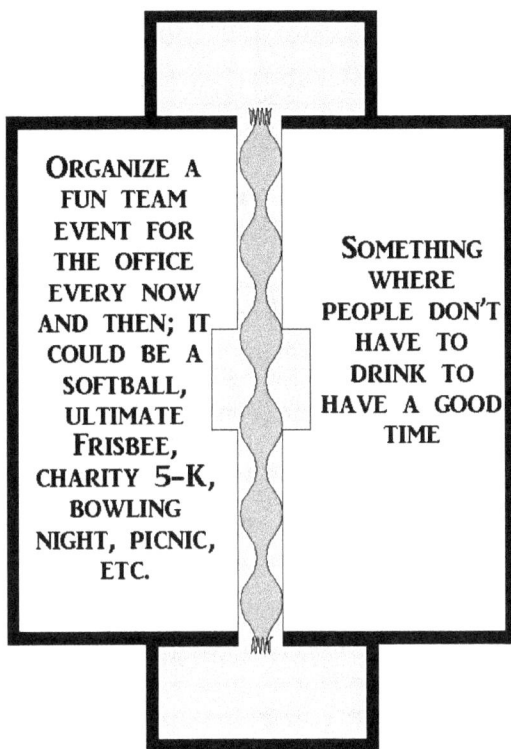

convicted, as they repeatedly moved for a mistrial during the proceedings and strenuously litigated against the State's case at every turn.

The State v. Anthony case just underscores, once again, without committing serious crimes, it is absolutely impossible to guarantee any result in litigation. This understanding needs to exist between attorneys and their clients. It is not as if the client is ordering a pizza from the lawyer, and the lawyer can guarantee that the client will get half-cheese, half-pepperoni, with a well-done bake, and that if the client doesn't like it the lawyer will make him a new one or give the client his money back. It is easy to feel that we can categorize, rate, arrange returns, and guarantee customer satisfaction for every single product, legal services included, in the marketplace of today, where business is increasingly conducted online and we want to use all of our devices to control and plot every aspect of our life.

But as of today, and until we can have computers perform lawyer functions, legal services cannot be rated and packaged like everything else. Much to everyone's dismay, there will always be that element of uncertainty and mystery about the legal world until computers have legal practice down to a science. With our advances in technology, that day very well could come in our lifetimes. But until then people need to get real about what customer service in the law really means, and every lawyer/client team should have this discussion and obtain a mutual understanding about this issue.

File Maintenance

With the advent of paperless filing and electronic documents, there are now more case management and filing options than ever. Many people still prefer a filing system consisting primarily of hard copies. There are of course advantages to a hard copy system; I personally find it is easier to read and digest a complex document that is in my hands, highlight it and make appropriate notes. Of course, there are now tools which allow one to mark up a document on screen, as with computer styluses, red-lining and comments. The many tools available now to create, read and edit documents are a matter of personal preference, but one thing everyone seems to agree on is having a system for protection of documents and data in case of disaster.

At my home office, I have used all-in-one printers/copiers/scanners for many years. My main problem with scanning documents on these machines, other than the limited speed, has been the size of the file to which the document is scanned. Before long, my computer began working like molasses because my file backups were fast using all its memory. Industrial machines not only work many times faster, but they also scan documents into files of only a few kilobytes, a drop in the bucket of an average computer's memory.

Over the years, with the progression of technology, the quality and relative affordability of office equipment has improved. My current home all-in-one will typically scan documents to PDFs of less than a gigabyte. As time goes on, we will surely continue to be able to store more and more data in less cyberspace. As it is now, I have all final/signed and draft copies of client documents backed up on my computer in relatively little space.

Some attorneys do not trust computerized or online file systems because they fear their system being hacked. Even as I maintain all my client files in cyberspace, I am fully aware that there is always a possibility that they could be hacked, just as it is always possible that a hacker could access systems of banks, government, even top secret defense and security data. This is the world we live in today; most people live at least some portion of their life online in modern times. This trend has not decreased, but only increased and expanded since the advent of the

Internet. There will always be risks. Even if one maintains only hard paper copies of files and keeps them under lock and key, there is always the possibility such files could be lost, stolen or destroyed. The infamous Hurricane Wilma left many businesses reeling for years as many lost all of their files and computer data in the storm.

Of course, office backup systems and technology are more sophisticated today than they were in 2005. Many offices use a combination of paper files and computer backup, but also expend thousands of dollars in storage space for files which could easily be kept online for free. Many businesses mistakenly think that they are required to keep hard copies of all documents, but many jurisdictions allow electronic storage only as proper maintenance of client files. Exceptions usually include extremely important or unique documents, such as physical evidence, negotiable instruments, wills and so forth.

But the majority of documents which populate client files, such as dockets, online public information, motions, pleadings, orders, calendars, contact information and billing can easily be maintained electronically with no necessity for an official paper file to ever be created. Temporary files could always be created when, for example, an assignment must be completed or documents are needed for court and hard copies of file documents are momentarily necessary or helpful. But after a particular assignment or hearing, file documents may not be needed again for months or even years. I find significant peace of mind in knowing that every single complete document in a case is safely preserved electronically, ready for me to print whenever I may need them. They are out of my way in the meantime, leaving my desk and cabinets clean and uncluttered.

Some people feel that a cluttered office is a sign of productivity; that mounds of papers and boxes of files in their office somehow indicate to observers that these workers are busy, not goofing off and are exempt from additional workload. I am against a disorganized working environment for several reasons. First, it can be difficult to locate items when one must sift through a pile of clutter first. Consequently, the aggregate time which one must spend sifting through such clutter builds up, until it equals countless billable hours lost per year.

Second, from my own experience, having an organized and tidy office can often be a cue to management that they can give you more work, since neatness somehow denotes that one has extra time on their hands. While office tidiness may have no actual relation to how busy one is, it is a sign of efficiency and productivity since, even though you may be under a number of pressing deadlines, you still care enough about your professional image and own standards to maintain an appearance of excellence as well. While at first, you may inwardly wince at the announcement that you are being assigned more files, you should always take the assignment of more work as a compliment. Additional work means that management has faith in your abilities to handle the volume with efficiency and accuracy, that you are recognized for your competence in the office, and perhaps best of all, that you are probably too valuable to lose. This knowledge can, if used appropriately, serve as valuable leverage if packaged the right way, in approaching conversations about raises and promotions.

On a brief secretarial temp assignment, I encountered one office which seemed to have the paperless filing system down pat. This office used Amicus Attorney as its case management platform. I had already become familiar with Amicus as the program had been included with our law school-laptops, and used the program for some simple organizational matters with both law school and work assignments. But Amicus had continued to evolve and by the time I took this assignment, Amicus conveniently took ownership of and organized every task and work product you might perform and complete in the office.

If you make a phone call pertaining to a case, a little memo form comes up where you can enter the case and matter number, telephone number, person called, and what the call is regarding. Once you dial, you can then start a timer which keeps track of the call length. Once your call is complete, you stop the timer and the program automatically calculates the number of hours you spend on the call and the amount you have billed. There is also a space for you to write your own notes about the call.

Whenever you write an email, prepare a document, take a phone message, schedule a calendar event, etc. in Amicus, they are assigned a case and matter number. When you look at any given case, the notes will automatically reflect all actions taken in the case, documents prepared, telephone calls, emails, and so forth in chronological order. This was invaluable to me in countless ways; perhaps most important of all was when a client called wanting to know the status of a matter. All I had to do was look at the notes in the opening screen and know exactly where the case stood; I could then give the client a timely update of what had been done, what was being done presently and what would happen next.

As with the Amicus phone memo feature, you could also use the billing timer while completing any task on a case. When beginning a task, you could start the timer and pause it when you had to pause or stop working on the project, know exactly how much you had honestly billed and be able to clearly explain to a client how your bill reflects only hours worked without any padding.

Also, once you scan in any document, you can then assign it an Amicus case name and matter number and it will automatically be included in that case's virtual library. When new mail came into that office, we would immediately scan it into Amicus, organize it alphabetically in an expando file, keep it for sixty days, then shred and discard it if the hard copy documents were no longer needed. Exceptions to this of course were certain documents, evidence materials, negotiable instruments, and other items where the original is available and is the best evidence.

If you want to get a simplified, streamlined paperless file system up and running in your office, Amicus is a great way to do it. It has always worked for me and I actually have more fun practicing law while using Amicus. I love the fact that I can go to the opening screen of the file and see each and every thing that was ever done on the file and when, in a neat little time line. I have had to read entire voluminous paper files, disorganized, with papers falling out left and right to try to decipher what is going on in the case. In comparison with that dreadful experience, Amicus is quite the drink of cool water.

Conclusion

The end goal for many attorneys is to have their own private practice, leveraging experience and skills learned as employees or simply diving into business ownership straight out of law school. As a business owner, there is no ceiling to your potential income, but there is also no floor. Business ownership often involves more risk than people are willing to assume, and so many opt into the seemingly more comfortable and stable life of an employee. Many people also do not believe they have the necessary entrepreneurial personality of a business owner.

However I believe that anyone can become a business owner, provided that they focus clearly on their unique talents and convert these into marketable services and/or products. At the same time, my purpose is not to dissuade people from pursuing a career in law or being an employee, but to provide some considerations I wish I had before pursuing my own future as an attorney.

Many attorneys I have met or known become extremely jaded, disillusioned, or burnt-out at some point in their career, including myself. Many of us launch into a legal career with grandiose visions, dreaming of a 100K-plus salary, prestige, fancy cars and houses, country clubs, respect, etc. Not all attorneys are rich and many struggle to make it, especially in our economy today. Fortunately, there is longevity in a legal career. It is one of the few vocations that computers cannot effectively replicate as of yet. In our age of streamlined, budget

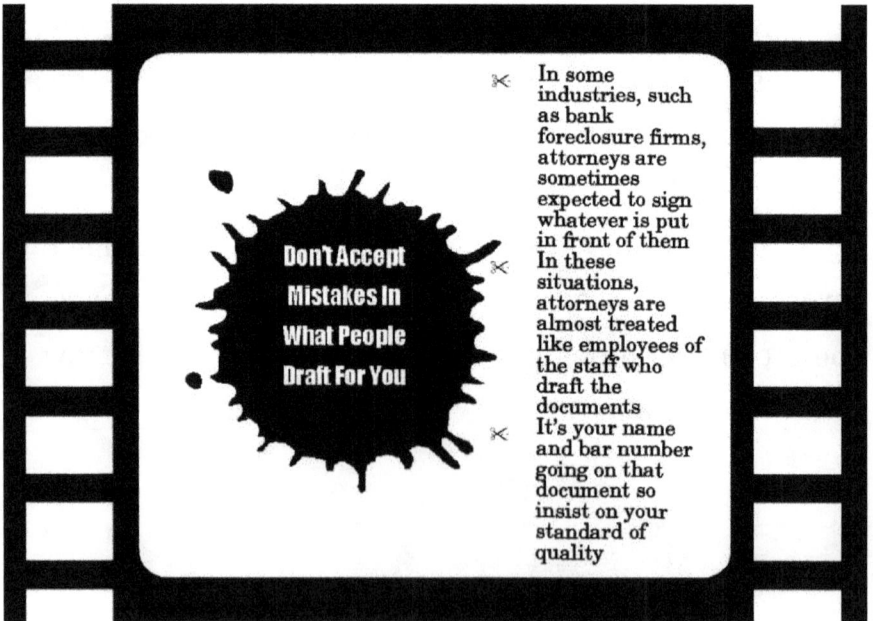

Don't Accept Mistakes In What People Draft For You

✂ In some industries, such as bank foreclosure firms, attorneys are sometimes expected to sign whatever is put in front of them

✂ In these situations, attorneys are almost treated like employees of the staff who draft the documents

✂ It's your name and bar number going on that document so insist on your standard of quality

workplaces much legal work is now farmed out overseas, such as clerical and support services, file maintenance, research and document preparation. However, nothing can substitute for admission to a state bar and license to practice law.

Our profession is constantly under siege by those engaged in the unlicensed practice of law, and those who would exploit lawyers for their own business purposes and financial gain.   Often, unlicensed individuals are caught handing out legal advice and preparing legal documents to those who are often too desperate to notice or care about the difference.

And the foreclosure default industry, at the end of the day, is primary controlled by non-lawyer bank executives and employees.   They hire attorneys to carry out their foreclosures and evictions, but the attorneys usually have no effective control over whether to settle a case or even to encourage same, or power to enjoin their clients from violating court rules and directives. Bank attorneys fervishly vie for default business and to keep cases in which the client's conduct would normally prompt their counsel to immediately withdraw. Foreclosure consultant scams often employ locally-licensed attorneys on whom the non-attorney masterminds can dump all the cases once they have collected the retainers from the clients, often making unfounded promises that the homes will be saved when more often than not, the homeowners will be left worse off than before.

Those who seek entry into the legal profession should be aware of the criticism individual lawyers face due to these assaults against the integrity of the legal profession, as well as other ethical violations and failures by some attorneys for which all lawyers seem to be blamed to some extent. Lawyers are often the butt of jokes in popular culture – some in good taste, some not. But when lawyers abide by the rules that govern our profession, represent their clients zealously and do their best work, these lawyers will likely reside highly in the opinion of their clients, the clients' family and friends, and gain professional recognition. Attorneys have the dubious honor of maintaining a profession in which it is almost possible to please everyone, but when they do please, they often do so on a momentous level.

I hope that this book has helped give direction to those who are considering legal careers, as well as lawyers who have already walked through the gates of bar admission. Of course, as in life, there are always things you must learn for yourself, but had I been introduced to many of these issues, or even thought to investigate them at a time I was perhaps not so blissfully ignorant, I would have done certain things differently. My wish for you is that you will be wiser, better informed and educated than I was when I embarked on my own legal career journey. And if you are already in the midst of that journey, perhaps further down the road than I, I hope you have found some useful nuggets here to simplify your career and life.